Immortal Gestures

Damon Young is a prize-winning philosopher and writer. He is the author or editor of fourteen books, translated into twelve languages. These include *On Getting Off*, *The Art of Reading*, *How to Think About Exercise*, *Philosophy in the Garden*, and *Distraction*. Damon has also written poetry, short fiction, and bestselling children's books.

Immortal Gestures

Journeys in the Unspoken

Damon Young

SCRIBE

Melbourne | London | Minneapolis

Scribe Publications
18–20 Edward St, Brunswick, Victoria 3056, Australia
2 John St, Clerkenwell, London, WC1N 2ES, United Kingdom
3754 Pleasant Ave, Suite 100, Minneapolis, Minnesota 55409, USA

Published by Scribe 2025

Copyright © Damon Young 2025

Illustrations by Angi Thomas

All rights reserved. Without limiting the rights under copyright reserved above, no part of this publication may be reproduced, stored in or introduced into a retrieval system, or transmitted, in any form or by any means (electronic, mechanical, photocopying, recording or otherwise) without the prior written permission of the publishers of this book.

The moral rights of the author have been asserted.

Typeset in Sabon by the publishers

Printed and bound in the UK by CPI Group (UK) Ltd, Croydon CR0 4YY

Scribe is committed to the sustainable use of natural resources and the use of paper products made responsibly from those resources.

Scribe acknowledges Australia's First Nations peoples as the traditional owners and custodians of this country, and we pay our respects to their elders, past and present.

978 1 925849 22 6 (Australian edition)
978 1 913348 55 7 (UK edition)
978 1 964992 08 2 (US edition)
978 1 761386 15 2 (ebook)

Catalogue records for this book are available from the National Library of Australia and the British Library.

scribepublications.com.au
scribepublications.co.uk
scribepublications.com

There is an old Buddhist adage: the teachings are like a finger pointing to the moon.

To achieve enlightenment, you are not supposed to look at the finger. You are supposed to look to the celestial light.

I am asking you to look at the finger. The finger is also the moon.

Tomorrow a child will put weight on his legs
for the first time. In an emergency
room someone will whisper a song once heard
by the last Mughal emperor, prayer of it
tuned to the splinter of a stone axe. Meanwhile
an anchorite, not knowing how to hold
his own hands, tends his dead mother's
garden, revealing its roots like burial
in reverse. But today you are the only living
thing in your apartment. You eat the peaches
I left in the crisper while you
watch the sun set, your body held
in the way some things are not like anything
else. Fifteen storeys below, my hand —
set in the same formation of bone by
which my ancestor, many mothers
ago, twisted passionfruit from the vine —
grips the doorknob that will bring me home.

                              Shastra Deo, 'Immortal Gestures'

Contents

Gobsmacked	1
Tally Up	20
Well? And? So?	32
Ply, Pliable, Pliant	45
Unclean, Undead	59
Fascinating	74
Horns	90
Pew Pew Pew	103
Shush	113
Gills, Glass	126
Savage Noble	136
Hello There	150
Aiki	163
Catching the Light	184
Hail	193
A Curt Nod	199
Gestures of Thanks	215

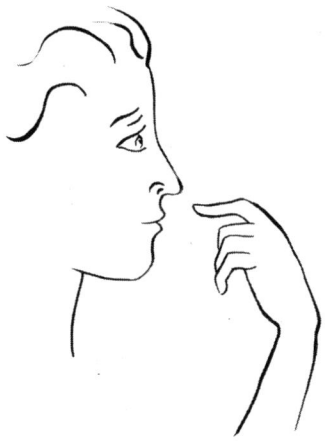

Gobsmacked

Look at him, this hesitant youth.

Almost nude, he stands in profile. His left leg is straight, right leg bent with his toes pointed down — as if he is about to take a step, but cannot. His eyes are wide, brows lifted. And witness: his finger is curled to his mouth.

This pausing boy invites my regard. I find him on a red-figure mixing jug from a Greek settlement in classical Italy. He is Herakles, the half god who became a full god in death. He is ageless and deathless now, a comely naïf.

That finger. That mouth. The god seems to be feeling surprise, bafflement, awe — perhaps all three. Why?

He is not astonished by his own nakedness, which is thoroughly Greek: the well-muscled physique, the dainty aristocratic penis. Not by his dandy lion-skin cloak, with the slain cat's mouth as his cowl — like the club in his left hand, this is typical Heraklean iconography. Not by Zeus and Victory looking down from the heavens, as he is shy of neither his father's gaze nor glory.

No, Herakles is taken aback by Herakles.

Standing in his own temple, he is looking at a stark white sculpture of himself being painted. (Thankfully, the hall is well lit. One night, the brute hurled a rock at his own statue, thinking it an enemy.) Seemingly for the first time, the god is witnessing his own image — and this image is more heroic than he. Mature in face and poised in posture, this Herakles stands in a confident contrapposto stance, with his club resting on a plinth. Our little god is amazed by this, his own stone self.

In this, the jug is art celebrating art. These Greeks did not believe that their statues were actually gods, that deities like Herakles were *in* the marble or bronze that portrayed them. Instead, the works mediated between deities and mortals. This was partly an aesthetic achievement, as statuary styles changed over the generations. Sculptures became less abstractly idealised, more nuanced and vivid. They offered the shock of perfection, as if the finest athletes existed in their splendour forever. Their beauty suggested divinity was near.

Perhaps some Greeks were anxious as statuary and sanctity parted ways, as the sculptures became just plain minerals or metals without some divine essence. If so, then this Herakles might have put them at ease. He showed them the awesome power of clay or pigment, guided by an artful hand.

After more than twenty-three centuries, this is partly what the young god is telling me with his pose: *I have been called here by this sublime statue. I strangled serpents in my crib, yet I am astonished by this work.* Meanwhile, the painter has his own proud message: *art is so commanding, even a deity is gobsmacked.*

Herakles praises fine art, yes. But he does so subtly, with a finger to his lips.

Brimming

See what began here, with just this small, brief movement? In fact, not even a movement — merely the artistic suggestion of it.

I start with an idea of Herakles' state of mind: cautious astonishment. Even if I know nothing about this youth, I see he is surprised and perhaps mystified. He is demonstrating what Charles Darwin called 'perplexed reflection', similar to someone cupping their chin or tugging their lip. Even putting aside the god's eloquent demeanour, this one gesture is enough for a basic feeling — a feeling we have in common, despite the millennia between us. The godling is taken aback by something unfamiliar, perhaps unusual.

To better understand his feeling, I look to his life: the stuff of Greek mythology. As a folk hero, Herakles is all over — and all over the place. He features in tales of handsome bravery and ugly madness, civilised generosity and gory violence. He is both the athlete who began the sacred Olympic games and a brute mocked for his hairy arse, both a philosopher and a killer. He is a man who suffers and dies, a god who exists forever on high, and perhaps something in between: a legendary striver who confronts and challenges death. In Buddhism, he becomes the bodhisattva Vajrapāṇi, club on his shoulder, ready to frighten away dogma and encourage enlightenment.

Even today, Herakles is a clumsy blue-eyed lunk in an animated musical and a savage hunk in a sword-and-sandals film; he is sweet, clumsy 'jerkules' or a swaggering, swearing mercenary ('fuck centaurs'). While some Greeks tried to neaten this mess, these contradictions were always part of the mythos. Whichever Herakles I choose, a duality exists there, an atmosphere of tension and conflict. It is no surprise that I find him puzzled on a jug, at once the awkward, goggling naïf *and* the cool, smouldering warrior.

And what did ordinary Greeks make of these red-figure divinities? If tragedy is any guide, they were most keen on Herakles as a symbol of pan-Hellenic heroism, as a familiar good guy whose ethnicity was simple and proud. Yes, he went mad and killed his own children, but those damned gods did it to him — he was a vulnerable champion, not a maniacal tyrant (a lie we still tell about men).

In this, the godling was perfect as decoration for ceramics, a harmless, friendly face to welcome the tired merchant into his apartment. Perhaps our amazed youth left his new owner with little more than the comfort of a well-painted celebrity, a star praising his own pretty likeness, finger to his lips.

So, I find Herakles' pose to be deceptively slight. Easily missed in a glance, it overflows with meaning: sympathetic feeling, ancient myths, Hellenic aesthetics and politics, colonial identities.

Gestures are like this: brimming.

To carry

Gestures are also often trivialised.

They are seen as furtive and partial, as not quite finished, as failed phrases. They are perhaps not real, and certainly not sincere. We 'gesture' at a problem instead of fixing it. The overall suggestion is obscurity, brevity, and superficiality.

Yet as Herakles shows, these slight movements carry immensities.

In fact, the word itself comes from the Latin 'gerĕre', which originally meant 'to carry'. We still speak of the way someone carries themselves, their proud or humble carriage. Observe the metaphor: as if they were schlepping themselves around, hefting bones and muscles. At its most basic, gesture simply refers to how we comport ourselves, to the flesh and its meaningful arrangements.

Put another way, gestures are behaviours that we notice — or should. This is not always because they are refined: the supplicant's praying hands, the archer's tense fingers. Instead, it is because they make the important manifest; they give the unusual but unseen a physical form. While some scholars are drawn chiefly to deliberate signs, our accidents are equally expressive.

Consider a black-figure painting of Herakles fighting the Nemean lion. There is no codified or customary gesture here, nothing especially pretty or intricate. His thick right leg is shoving backwards against the dirt, his arms clasped around the cat's throat. This is obviously pragmatic, as there are only so many ways to grapple a huge beast. Yet this practical pose still suggests a story. The hero must strangle the lion because its hide cannot be cut; this killing must happen because King Eurystheus ordered him to do so; the king commanded the hero because Hera made sure Eurystheus was born first; Hera loathed Herakles because his father Zeus screwed yet another mortal; and so on, until we end up back at Hesiod's primordial 'chaos ... first of all'. Even the most unmannered and untaught movements speak to what was. We are quite literally creatures of history: we are created by it, just as we create it.

Because history is not random, gestures often mark our social position. Herakles is no oik. His bearing is that of a well-fed, well-trained aristocratic Greek, someone who had the finest schooling in archery, boxing, lyre, augury. He was able to gratify his famously huge appetites for wine, grub, and fifty princesses. (The cartoon lunk is allowed one chaste kiss.) As sociologist Pierre Bourdieu observes, society literally informs our bodies in this way: it gives them form. From our manners of flirtation, to the sports we play, to our swagger as we stand on a plinth, we are conditioned by class and status. Punishment and reward, confinement and relative freedom, shame and celebration — all these are used to train the flesh.

My point is not to reduce all behaviour to politics or economy, to make nonsense of our individuality. Instead, my point is to show how our gestures are not wholly *ours*. We are taught how to move, and often why; we learn how to express ourselves with pointing or shrugging — or when to stay still. No private language exists, for we always arrive in a universe shot through with communication. This is as true for gesture as it is for my English or Herakles' classical Greek.

This is why our youthful god did not need to first think of his puzzlement, then painstakingly translate this into a finger to his lips. His gesture *was* the feeling of amazement. Likewise, had Herakles been furious, he would have not needed to sit and consider the right signs — he would have simply grimaced, then put up his pugilistic fists. And anyone who understood these gestures would have done so straightforwardly. 'The gesture does not make me think of anger,' wrote philosopher Maurice Merleau-Ponty, 'it is anger itself.'

Because of this, gestures can be instantly affecting. They reveal someone's state of mind to me, often without me being aware of it. They suggest nascent ideas, nod to spatial cues, press home important points. If Herakles were speaking English to me, gestures might even help me listen through his thick accent. The gist is there, and it is swift and visceral. Delightfully, dogs on ancient Greek ceramics still have the same familiar poses as today, and as animals we have our own instinctual signs of aggression or submission.

But we are not hounds. For all their poignancy and sway, our movements are highly contextual. While some of their categories can be generalised, gestures themselves arise from specific times and places. This is why the ancients sometimes misunderstood or misreported their own statues. One city's artwork was quite foreign to the next, despite common deities and heroes. This is to say nothing of the later Romans or much later Anglophones, heirs to centuries or millennia of inventions. Being situated is our lot, and our gestures rarely make sense without these situations.

To complicate things even more, many gestures are not encountered directly. I never met our Herakles, nor did any of the classical Greeks. He was painted on baked clay. Vases and bowls were often decorated with drama, offering buyers recognisable stories. Yet tragedy itself took poses from ceramics for its theatrical language. So gestures floated to and fro within the currents of several arts, never being found outside the waters of specific significance. Perhaps some merchants gained their heroic manners from pottery, and not the other way around. While I write here of gestures' immediacy, they are always mediated. *We* are always mediated.

Herakles is eternally a beautiful youth, his look of surprise outliving him by many centuries. His immortal gesture conveys his mood to me with fleetness and vivacity. I feel like I know him, with his hesitant feet and halted finger. But his pose cannot contain all of his world; it fails to reveal its own origins, in a workshop in Italy's Hellenic heel.

Gestures are vast, but elusive in this very vastness. They invite attention but also study — intellectually, we have to carry what they cannot. We cannot carry them as they do, but this is how scholarship works. We grasp carefully, patiently what we usually lug around thoughtlessly.

Continuum

There is much to carry.

Because gestures are a tightly packed jumble, I want to lighten my load. Thankfully, scholar Adam Kendon provided a useful way to sort the various kinds, an innovation later called 'Kendon's continuum'.

Think of this as a line running horizontally. On the far left are what Kendon calls 'gestures' and others 'gesticulations'. These are spontaneous, typically used alongside speech, rarely put together to make phrases, and done off the cuff. Think of pointing at a mixing bowl and saying 'old mate is wrestling a cat'. I might point with a thumb, one or two fingers, my chin, my elbow. Either way, this conveys what the words do not: it is *that* guy who has his arms around the lion. Once this is done, no more gestures are needed for now, and speech continues until the next hand flick, twirl, or shake.

In the middle of the continuum are emblems and pantomimes. Emblems are also called 'Italianate gestures', because they are often more in your face in the Mediterranean. Think of a ring made with the thumb and forefinger: unless you are a white supremacist, it typically just means 'okay'. In Plato's time, it was instead a profession of love. These gestures are not languages; they have semantics, but no syntax. They are used here and there instead of speech, they are well known in a community, and they have standards. Like silent phrases, they can be performed well, poorly, or not at all — an 'okay' sign that looks like a fist is literally just a fist. Emblems used alongside speech are what some call 'recurrent gestures'. These have a common basic meaning, but are variable in context. Think of someone holding up their open palm while chatting: this might easily be a casual shrug or an earnest entreaty.

Pantomime often takes the place of speech, but chiefly through likeness and movement. We try to make our hands look like whatever we are portraying: strangling a big cat, skinning its hide, putting this on as a cape. Like language, there is an order here — typically one of narrative, one thing after another — but no code. Pantomime does not stand for things, it apes them.

On the continuum's far right are sign languages,

which are systematised, can be used without a word being spoken aloud, and have well-known standards of style, grammar, and so on. Plato described the beginnings of this in his *Cratylus*, perhaps written while the Herakles mixing jug was being painted. 'Suppose that we had no voice or tongue, and wanted to communicate with one another,' he wrote. 'Should we not ... make signs with the hands and head and the rest of the body?' Plato's description is deceptive. It suggests that signing is compensatory, merely the second-best option if speech is lost or never gained. Signing *is* language. It gestures with the hands as speakers do with their tongues and lips.

Importantly, this is a continuum of categories, not things; and the categories are blurred, not fine. Herakles might mimic himself chopping a Hydra's neck, or he might slice his hand in the air for silence. The first is pantomime, the second a metaphorical gesticulation about the conversation itself — the two gestures are exactly the same. Gestures arise from changeable psyche and society, and share in this mercuriality. They are a dense miscellany.

This kind of escapee

I am drawn to gestures that drag stories with them.

Because of this, I am more interested in emblems or pantomimes than in fleeting flicks, jabs, or wiggles. I recognise that these spontaneities are vital in our shared lives, but they are too idiosyncratic and ephemeral for my tastes. The more communal, continuing movements like Herakles' invite me to tease out their histories, and I cannot feign interest elsewhere.

I am led by curiosity. As David Hume defined it so neatly, this is the gift of enjoying intellectual labour. We 'fix our attention or exert our genius', he wrote, and find this 'pleasant and agreeable'. We cannot do so randomly — the exercise must be challenging, and it helps to believe in its worth. Also, Hume was not arguing that we *must* be this way, that there is some ethical duty to flex our minds. He was simply observing that so-called 'pure' curiosity is misnamed and misleading. We get pleasure from sweating intellectually; we are partisans for quiet joy.

One of the benefits of curiosity is illuminating possibilities beyond comfortable actuality. The here and now has a charm to it; the charisma of the obvious, which prompts no second-guessing. Curiosity nudges me to look past this stubborn fact and see how the rest of the world is quietly implicated in my life. This is a basic philosophical endeavour, enlarging our conception of common reality.

Think of Herakles. In the European world at least, we all know his name, even if Latinised as Hercules. He is the stuff of easy familiarity: drawn, acted, chiselled, etched, sung, danced. As a classical Greek and Roman character, he has become our own — he is part of a loose but large canon, which continues century to century. At the very least, the hero is a nod-on-the-street acquaintance, easily portrayed by a bodybuilder or wrestler, easily equipped with a wooden sword, loincloth, and a little dubbing. Just the name is enough: there are Hercules dog chews and cat litter trays, Hercules calmatives and laxatives.

Yet it takes only a little prying to discover how odd Herakles was, with his lion for a cape and cowl; how alien his Hellenic world was, with its god-beckoning statuary. A familiar stranger.

We are all Herakles in this respect, surrounded by forgotten foreignness. We have to work to discover how our little universe makes sense. Alfred North Whitehead believed this was the very definition of philosophy, and why he called my vocation a 'critic of abstractions'. The problem is not abstractions, as we need these to make sense of the world. The problem is forgetting that they *are* abstractions. Our visions of existence are partial, jaundiced by interest, and not entirely our own. We are not transcendent gods. We arrive in an already-wrought society, and its patina of normality is often entrancing.

Just as importantly, we tend to believe in the obviousness of the clear and distinct. We ignore the wide weave of things in favour of a few large knots. Whitehead phrased it this way, quoting a poem by John Milton: 'The concentration of attention upon matter-of-fact is the supremacy of the desert. Any approach to such triumph bestows on learning "a fugitive, and a cloistered virtue".'

I chase gestures to avoid being this kind of truant.

Flesh

I am keen on the body.

This might seem like another partiality — after all, a body wrote this. But European philosophers have a history of vilifying, mocking, or simply overlooking corporeality. Taking thought as the best of our humanity, they have caricatured the flesh as what weakens, distracts, or misleads us. For Plato, the body was famously a jail or weight, from which the soul had to flee. With a few notable exceptions, Christian theologians were Platonists of a stripe. They were cautious of the corpus at best, scornful at worst.

For seventeenth-century thinker René Descartes, the body was a lump of stuff with which the mind was lumped. He recognised that these were somehow united, but fervently fantasised otherwise. His philosophy arose from the fiction of spirit wholly purified of its matter: a mental substance as against a physical substance. Yet in arguing for an ethereal soul, he used material metaphors, like the 'foundations' of knowledge. These tropes only made sense from within a palpable self and world. While philosophy has recently welcomed the flesh once again, Cartesian dreams are still very common.

My interest in gestures is part of a modern renaissance of the corporeal. Here, the body is many things: a biological organism, a lived to and fro with the world, a form of human intimacy, a cultural artefact. To look more closely at any gesture is always to see corporeality as well. This is not simply in the pointing finger, but in the shared life in which pointing makes sense.

So my ideal here is receptivity, becoming more aware of our inevitable and intricate participation in a colossal world. To do this, we must think of the mind, not as an aloof alien observer, but as an achievement. We do not have minds, we *mind*. And this endeavour arises from — with, in, as, through — physical existence. This is why Merleau-Ponty called flesh 'the darkness needed in the theatre to show up the performance'.

Put another way, Plato was almost correct: we cannot escape bodies. This is not because they are prisons, but because even our supposed escape is through bodies.

Gestures highlight this corporeality. They give language an objective character by making objects of our ideas and feelings: a finger pressed to lips, a clenched fist, a bent knee. They toy with imagined stuff, which is picked up, stretched, thrown, handed over. They allow us to feel how the everyday shapes us in this sore muscle group, that tight tendon. This is one of the benefits of yoga, encouraging a scrutiny of the self — like a god inspecting his own statue. In a world where words are spiritualised as mere information, gestures invite a similar inspection.

Kairos

I am also curious about time. Or, rather: timing.

To speak of time typically suggests clocks, the ticks that punctuate our days. But this is only one kind of temporality, arising chiefly in the European Enlightenment. It came to dominate during the Industrial Revolution and was as much economic and political as scientific. Mapping and colonising new territories, securing routes of trade and conquest, controlling factories — these all required precise timekeeping. Clocks enabled not only more efficient cycles of production, distribution, and consumption, but also labour itself: a universal time of hours worked and wages paid. Highly abstract time came to be ordinary.

My point is not that abstract time is somehow fake. It is quite real and very powerful. It shapes our common history (or lack of it). My point is that clock time is only one temporality among various: biological, psychological, social, aesthetic. These can certainly be measured with a chronometer. But their basic logics are not clockwork; they have their own cadences and beats.

This is why some philosophers discuss 'human time'. Not because capitalism is not human, but because we have our own innate and intuitive temporalities. As German philosopher Edmund Husserl observed, consciousness is not a sequence of thing-like 'nows', but a continuous reach forward and back. We pull the past along with us as we hurl a future ahead of us. And we do this for the immediate 'now' and 'then' as much as for ancient history or far-flung futures. Well before we made clocks, we made time.

This creation is worldly, because we are not aloof timekeepers. We exist in a definite here and now, with definite urges and ideals. We are always grasping at circumstances, literally and figuratively. This is why John Dewey discussed 'experience'. It is not some private play in our minds, but a continuing congress with a world that matters to us. Giving and receiving, doing-to and being-done-to, seeking and withdrawing — we are part of a rhythmic whole.

When our tempos combine with those of the world, we have a kairos. From the Greek, this is what Aristotle called 'the right time'. Perhaps a young man when our Herakles bowl was painted, the famed sculptor Lysippos crafted a personification of Kairos: a winged youth carrying scales and a razor. The first suggests weighing up the perfect moment, the other this moment's thinness. Bald but for a single forelock by his temple, Kairos seems to be alighting briefly on his toes before leaping away. The god's hair must be seized while he is passing, or he will be gone forever. We see the youth approaching and we grab him — or we do not. No o'clock can be agreed upon beforehand; we only have our judgement. This can be translated into some general metric, but not performed through it. Kairos is a hard-won knack for timeliness.

Gestures are all about this kind of timing. This is partly because they are often partnered with talk: emphasising, complementing, replacing. We do not throw out our hands haphazardly. We fit them neatly to our spoken phrases, typically one for each clause. We move easily from signing about things to signing about the words for things, from my viewpoint to yours. These movements can allow dualities to linger, with one idea in speech and another in a shaking fist or pinched thumb and forefinger. We hang on to hesitant solutions that would otherwise be dropped.

Yet gestures need not be paired with speech like this. They can communicate enough alone, when they are sensitive to the kairos.

Perhaps I am walking in a sanctuary and come across a beautiful statue. Then I recognise it as myself. I cannot find the words for this sublime moment — and speech might profane the silence anyway. Instead of stuttering or mumbling, I put a finger to my lips. The touch comforts me enough to relax and reflect, but also symbolises my amazement. I give physical form to my own state of mind, and to the world in which I stand gawping: aristocratic, devotional, artistic.

Gestures are the tangible culminations of a living tempo. They do away with anaemic formality.

The sea! The sea!

I have offered my philosophical rationale here. Through gestures, I am drawn to a more stretched existence, to what Whitehead called the 'vague "beyond", waiting for penetration in respect to its detail'. But is my penetration really moved by curiosity alone?

To begin, a caution: authors are often the last to know why a work is what it is. They tell tales to themselves and others; they play sage or raconteur or clown; they find agreeable or just saleable origin stories. But their true urges and ideals are often opaque to them; or they are transparent, but shameful or dull.

I grant this. I am wary of the literary mythos.

But if I can write honestly of myself, perhaps I am lonely. Perhaps my recent life — grief and its anxieties, chronic and acute ills, global plague, literary collapse, all on a small unloved island off a large unloved island — perhaps my recent life has left me feeling estranged. I find myself small and weak and slight and out of reach. From what? From wherever are consolation and comfort.

Legend has it that Herakles adored a hot soak. After his travels, he swam and scrubbed himself in steaming waters. In Sicily, 'the Nymphs caused warm baths to gush forth so that he might refresh himself after the toil sustained in his journeying'.

Perhaps I am bathing myself therapeutically in the waters of a larger world. I am not so much trying to be clean, as hoping to be enveloped: immersed in something bigger than myself. It is soothing to float, even if the tides are so very human.

Yes, philosophy is not therapy. While it helped Seneca to slit his wrists calmly in his bath, it drowns as often as it buoys. It can depress, disorient, paralyse. It can even bore. I am not under any illusion here. Truth is not my medicine.

Nonetheless, perhaps part of this work is me trudging over the sands, then diving in and down. Perhaps I am calling out like Xenophon's ten thousand mercenaries, finally sighting the coast after years of marching: 'The sea! The sea!'

Ketos

So, I am exploring how gestures are more expansive and enduring than they seem — how *we* are more expansive and enduring than we seem. That is to say, I am thumbing my nose at petty ideas of our existence.

This can be overwhelming, as the links between gestures and stories make a great chain of becoming. Once this kind of thinking begins, it can be a trial to slow or stop. The associations lead to associations lead to associations — and so on. This can be frightening, even to scholars.

Herakles once slew Ketos, a sea monster. Romanised as Cetus — whence we have 'cetacean' — this was something between a whale, a serpent, a dragon, a big fish. Whatever it was, this beast was about to eat Hesione, a princess from Troy. Herakles went to work. But instead of simply clubbing or cutting Cetus, he allowed himself to be swallowed by it. Then he hacked his way out, killing the monster from within.

I occasionally sympathise with Herakles, falling into the enormity of gestures, into something much larger and more primal than myself. Though perhaps Herakles himself is the gesture, and I am Cetus. Having roamed the world and become many things, the wrecker lives violently in me — and I suddenly find myself spread out most messily. Perhaps there is no Ketos, but the Hydra instead: two new meanings facing me as soon as one is cut away. Or perhaps my psyche is merely the Augean stables and gestures the flood, clearing away my mind's dung. See? More associations.

For all this drama, my labours here are not heroic. I am more like the farmer Herakles once sat with, who told the slayer mock-epic tales of killing mice. I offer no great new theory of gesture — I labour gratefully with the work of others. I provide no encyclopaedia or dictionary, which lists examples: an exhaustive alphabet of palms, fingers, thumbs. Instead, I choose those movements that most interest me, that retain and reward my curiosity, that suggest something much more than themselves. I look to literature, popular culture, my own life. And I draw on various disciplines — from philosophy to history, psychology to sociology, anthropology to archaeology — to make sense of these. Or more correctly, to make sense of how these make sense.

I am not Herakles. But I am staring at him staring, my finger also to my lips. Join us.

Tally Up

You are eating in a restaurant. The food is enjoyable. The decor is enjoyable. The company is enjoyable. You are safe and stimulated. You are in a good conversation, though only just: you have to lean forward to be heard.

Still talking, you finish your meal, put down your cutlery, and gain a server's eye. Then you raise your hand and move it slightly. The waiter understands. They bring a small piece of paper on a tray. It lists your food and drink and their total cost. You pay this, then leave.

This is not your experience. Or, rather: this is a vague abstraction of your experience and others'. It is form, designed for your content.

Perhaps the restaurant is Greek, and you are eating fasolada under a pergola. The evening is warm, the beer cold. English tourists are asking if they can drink on the streets. There is a piglet running between tables.

Perhaps the restaurant is Korean, and you are eating bibimbap in a booth near the wet windows. There is a giant robot with an equally giant mace painted in acrylics on the wall. At a table nearby, children are grilling strips of beef; toddlers are wriggling on the vinyl cushions.

Perhaps the restaurant is Indonesian, and you are eating tempeh over Formica. While you sip teh manis, men beside you are arguing about football. Wearing large black headphones, the owners' daughter is drawing a fluorescent-pink horse in thick lines.

For each — and for countless others in countless other countries — you will attract the waiter's attention in the same way: twirling your thumb, forefinger, and middle finger together, either in the air at the server or towards your own palm. That is to say, you will mime handwriting. The waiter will then give you your bill.

Writing

This 'cheque please' gesture is peculiar.

You typically feign writing to suggest — writing. Symbolically, the hand and pen mean prose or poetry. Despite the ubiquity of buttons and screens, we still associate manuscripts with what is 'manū scrīptus', written by hand. This is partly because of skeuomorphism, old iconography making new technology seem familiar. On our digital devices, icons of pens or brushes replace the physical things. And this makes sense, because most of us still become literate while holding a crayon, chalk, pen, pencil.

But suppose you are in an eatery, writing. Your pen is dry, or your pencil snaps, or your page is soaked with coffee. So you ask the server for pen and paper. Do you just raise your hand and mime scribbling? No, because here the usual iconography pauses. It is not that composing at table is somehow freakish, but that it is not the default here; there is no shorthand for longhand. You have to use words rather than the usual emblem; you must articulate, not gesticulate.

This is because the 'cheque please' movements are not about ordinary writing. They are about adding up. While the gesture might suggest a signature, it was established before the widespread use of credit cards internationally. And the 'cheque' here is a bill of sale, not a signed cheque. The gesture is also used for cash payments, which need no authorisation at all. It is the wordless equivalent of this phrase: *please prepare your bill and bring it to me.*

In the very early twentieth century, Henry James did not describe the movement made in *The Ambassadors*, but it certainly worked as ours does: 'He had signed to the waiter that he wished to pay.' Likewise in Virginia Woolf's *The Waves*:

> The handsome young man in the grey suit ...
> with a characteristic gesture at once commanding
> and benign, made a sign to the waiter, who came
> instantly and returned a moment later with the
> bill discreetly folded upon a plate.

For well over a century, we have been briefly, silently asking waiters to tally for us.

Interestingly, this points to the very origins of writing. When script first arose in Mesopotamia — almost three millennia before Plato warned us about it — it came from trade. Clay tokens were used to represent goods like grain, livestock, oil. These were put into ceramic containers, which were later marked for easy calculation. Eventually, these marks were enough, and they came to mean abstract numbers: like twoness in general, rather than simply two things. This principle was then extended to likenesses: pictures, which meant things rather than just amounts. Soon, the pictograms for things were gathered to sound out words. Suddenly — that is, within centuries — the city-state of Ur had writing, and it was rendering law, history, and poetry rather than just recording stock.

So, commerce to writing to commerce. Your gesture is something of a strange loop of symbolism.

Dénouement

Note the timing of your movements too.

They happen once the meal has ended — perhaps after dessert, but before the various goodbyes. Or more correctly, they do not so much happen as *make* happen. Gesturing for the cheque is not simply a statement of a want, the public report of a private fact. It helps to bring about the evening's dénouement; it concludes, rather than simply occurring at the conclusion.

In this, it is what philosopher John Austin called 'performative': a communication that accomplishes things in being communicated. It cannot be judged true or false — this is a category mistake. It *does*. And what the 'cheque please' sign does is not simply to summon the bill, but to end the dinner. Even if intimates, friends, or colleagues want to continue eating, this meal — this unique event, with its own atmosphere and rhythm — is over. You have brought it to a close with a few wrist whirls.

But why use a gesture at all?

Babel and bubbles

The 'cheque please' sign can often be compensation: for incomprehension, incapacity, inattention.

Ideally, it is a courtesy to learn a little of the local language. But life is not ideal. There are not enough hours to pick up Greek and Korean and Indonesian; or you are ill or old; or you are simply a colonial, whose global dominance leaves you a thick-tongued provincial. Whatever your reasons or excuses, you find yourself asking for the cheque in a foreign country. And so you do something seemingly strange, but helpfully common: you write with pretend ink on pretend paper with a pretend pen. The server turns to the counter for you.

And even if you do know the tongue, you might not be able to speak and be heard. A throng of diners all talking at once can be as loud as traffic — then add muzak and echoing walls. Or your waiter's ears are not what they once were. Or your first language is sign, and you are weary of always translating. Whether done slyly or with a flourish, this gesture easily takes the place of talk.

Yet you might speak the lingo fluently, find yourself a hushed nook — and *still* prefer to gesture. Perhaps the waiter is lurching from table to table, kitchen to courtyard, and you want to pay. So you find just the right moment — their head is turned, their eyes up — to wave and sign. You recognise that they are busy and you want them busy *with you*.

Or perhaps you just want conversation, so you withdraw from waitstaff, other patrons, ambient patter. As Erving Goffman observed, you are now in a bubble of sorts, which only allows certain stimuli through its membrane. You ignore nearby tiffs, sudden cackles, smashing glasses — all to keep that thin, translucent film around you. Despite knowing exactly what to say to the garçon, you instead wiggle your drawn-together fingers: you do not want your tête-à-tête to pop.

The monster

So, the 'cheque please' gesture has various causes. Yet it always has one expected effect: service.

Suppose you gesture this way at your friend's kitchen table. They would understand you well enough, but they would also be confused. Even if the meal were a calculated gift, your movements would be absurd: one does not provide a bill for a home-cooked meal.

This is because your mate's free labours are what Marx called 'unproductive'. The German philosopher's point was not that hospitality is a waste: he enjoyed a pint or eighteen when finances allowed. Marx's point was that *any* labour for capitalists is unproductive if it is not making money.

In bourgeois society, waiters do not exist only to bring plates, glasses, and bills to patrons. They also exist to bring profit to bosses. The latter have the assets: the ingredients, the stoves to cook them in, the tables to serve them on. The former have nothing but themselves: hands to carry trays, backs to stoop over tables, smiling eyes to make customers feel doted-upon.

So serving staff toil for payment. This payment is spent keeping themselves and their families breathing: on shelter, sustenance, clothing. But workers are not paid all they make for businesses. Bosses take extra for themselves, what Marx called 'surplus-value', or profit. With this, employers buy more stuff: ingredients, stoves, tables. They also buy more labour, with which they turn their stuff into goods and services.

Capital makes capital makes capital. This is why Marx called capital 'a live monster that is fruitful and multiplies'.

As Marx's metaphor suggests, this is not a natural relationship, not something we can discover in field trips or biology textbooks. It is executed socially, perhaps first requiring heads to roll. And even when peaceful and cheery, it is a kind of power — *the* kind of power in capitalist cultures. Marx put it neatly:

> Capital is thus the *governing power* over labor and its products. The capitalist possesses this power, not on account of his personal or human qualities, but inasmuch as he is an *owner* of capital. His power is the *purchasing* power of his capital, which nothing can withstand.

And how does this governor rule? With haste.

When the modern restaurant began in eighteenth-century Paris, one of its innovations was timing. You no longer dined arse-by-arse with strangers, arriving for a common course; no longer banqueted together on benches; no longer ate what the hotelier happened to have in the larder. Instead, you sat at your little table in your little room. And you chose exactly the meal you wanted, exactly when you wanted it. For you: the public performance of private choice. For the establishment: cycle after cycle of service.

It is no coincidence that the restaurant was a bourgeois innovation. Capital must keep circulating, but there are pauses between making and using, producing and consuming: 'It must spend some time as a cocoon before it can take off as a butterfly.' The capitalist tries to hasten this pupa. The more commodities made and sold every hour, the greater his profit. The greater the profit, the more he can invest. With more investment, more commodities can be made and sold, more cheaply and quickly. And so it begins again. This happens globally, as planetary systems allow for instant calculation and control. It also happens locally in your eatery as the boss rushes through as many diners as physiology, etiquette, and branding allow.

Because of this, many waiters lack the freedom to slow down or speed up as they please, to seek needful conversation or equally needful rest. As Marx noted, capital has a 'were-wolf hunger for surplus-labour', which has nothing to do with health or liberty. Often young and low-paid, servers are hired to keep throughput high. It is their job to make sure the customer pays their bill and another customer quickly takes their place. And if the server fails? Another young and low-paid worker can quickly take *their* place.

So, your quick sign to a server need not be about your interests — and certainly not about theirs. Often, it is the boss who most benefits: fast waiters fill his wallet. In this, it neatly reflects the economic status quo, feeding Marx's monster as you feed yourself.

And if the 'cheque please' is less popular now, perhaps this monstrous reality is why. It is not simply because of scannable codes and phone payments — the sign has survived cheques and coins and cards. Instead, it is because this gesture seemingly belongs to the entitled elderly, comfortable with their hands on the high rungs of capital's ladder.

Want

Perhaps you grumble at my emphasis on capitalism; you say I am being cynical at best, conspiratorial at worst. Hospitality, you mutter, is more than commodities.

I certainly hope so. Even the most basic use value — food as useful calories and nutrients — can typically be found in a restaurant, offering something other than exchange value.

More importantly, there are kinds of worth that resist the tightening bonds of capital altogether: ethical, political, aesthetic. Individually, there are virtues of hospitality, like liberality and patience. Communally, there are ancient customs that guide host and guest, citizen and stranger, transforming the dangerous alien into the known familiar.

There can also be more liberated institutions, which stand for values other than the market. Here as in other industries, eateries work against the logic of dollar-store liberalism. 'We can and must intervene in the world of politics,' Pierre Bourdieu once said, 'but with our own means and ends.' For some, these means and ends are a welcoming meal.

But if these endeavours succeed, it is only because we are wise to bourgeois ideology. One of capital's oldest ruses is to deny or trivialise the economy, to pretend that its rationality is innocent or irrelevant. The more it achieves this pretence, the less the world seems capitalist at all — it is just what is. The fantasy of matter-of-fact.

As a diner, you often *want* this pretence. You enjoy being liberated from workaday necessity. Liberation might be a brief break from shopping, cooking, cleaning: the dull entropic parade of the domestic carnival. It might be connoisseurship, savouring subtle or vivid gastronomy for its own sake. Either way, eateries can pause your labours.

Yet they do not offer this emancipation to the waiter, who is paid to serve their employer by serving you. It is the market that affords you a holiday from the market. It is a real vacation, but not from society itself. (Durkheim: 'God is society.')

Your raised hand is not so elevated that it transcends the bourgeois universe.

Stuck

Now suppose you again gesture this way at your friend's kitchen table — after an acquaintance has said something absurd. Perhaps they are proud capitalists, opining on the laziness of the poor, on the welcome correlation of talent, labour, and success. (This one neat trick: be born to wealthy parents, who were born to wealthy parents.) Rather than haranguing them, you simply show a nonexistent waiter that you want to pay the nonexistent bill.

Ha.

The guests laugh, because they feel your sentiment immediately. You are not communicating that you actually want to pay, or even that you actually want to end the conversation. Your gesture might be your first reply of many — the derision before the dispute. Instead, you are using the 'cheque please' movement as an analogy for your state of mind: *I feel like someone who wants to surreptitiously flee an awkward meal in a restaurant.*

Note the levels of significance here. Previously, you wrote with pen and paper. Then you faked holding a pen and paper, but sought a real server and cheque. Now every part of the movement is purely theatrical. The physicality is roughly the same, but its category has changed: from the practical, to the metonymic, to the metaphorical. Yet all the guests get it.

Aristotle observed that metaphor is a kind of born talent, a bent that works beneath technique. It allows the artist to see unexpected likenesses between the unlike. If the philosopher is right, this gift is celebrated because we *all* seek these tropes, because our minds work by pushing and stretching notions beyond their origins. Friedrich Nietzsche: 'Every concept arises from the equation of unequal things.' This is why everyone understands your joke effortlessly: writing, eatery, waiter, and what these say about your state of mind.

They also know to find it witty — or at least know that you are trying. (Waiters are sometimes paid to smile at your jokes. Friends are not.) They see the humour in your juxtaposition: a market gesture at a domestic table. You wish you could end things like a paying diner, but you cannot.

In this, your gag is recognition of a common

existence. You are stuck with equals, and not merely with employers and employees.

Back to it

You are writing at a café on the weekend. Fingers not yet cramping around the pen, your phrase is almost finished: *Your raised hand is not so elevated that it transcends the bourgeois* —

In her generic livery — black slacks, black shirt, sensible shoes — the waitress brings your jam shortbread and coffee. 'It's so lovely out here. I wish I could just sit in the sun.' Her hand rises slowly then falls quickly, seemingly describing the fantasy's plausibility. 'Well. Back to it,' she says, walking quickly inside.

You get back to it.

— *universe.*

Well? And? So?

'Cain rose up against Abel his brother, and slew him.'

How familiar Cain's crime is: another young man killing another young man. Another brother killing a brother. Coveting his Father's praise, Cain commits the very first murder. We understand his envy if not his rage: Daddy, what about *me*?

A noir moment: God asks the criminal where his brother is. Perhaps staring into the light that is his Father, the criminal replies with that famously disingenuous phrase of disavowal: 'I know not. Am I my brother's keeper?'

He *is* his brother's keeper, as are we all. (This is morality.) And he *does* know where Abel is — as does God. The corpse is where Cain left it, bleeding into the dirt. The criminal will not show his guilt, though; he will not weep and whine (yet). He tries to deceive God, of all beings.

But Cain's statement is less about where Abel is, and more about what Abel means to him. He is not simply saying that he does not know. He is saying that he does not *care*, that his brother is nothing to him.

While the scriptures have their poetic phrases, they are not novelistic. They do not describe what the criminal does as he lies to furious omniscience. Perhaps he cringes. Perhaps he scowls. But I cannot see the fratricide as doing anything other than shrugging. Aching from the pickaxe, Cain's farmer's shoulders are lifted; calloused from the plough, his palms are raised.

In later Jewish commentaries, Cain advertises his own naivety. This was literally the first death and the first homicide. 'Did you even tell me that, if I struck him, he would die?' Surely the son of Adam shrugged as he said this.

Why would he shrug? Because it is what I would do.

He does what he wills

God does not shrug.

He rages, yes — turning cities to ash and a loved one to salt. His wrath is there from the beginning. And if he does not smile with pleasure, he is certainly pleasable: before the torture and murder begin, he judges the world good. God also loves. While he is more ethereal sprite than man, he offers intimacy. 'Who will grant me that you come to my heart and intoxicate it,' wrote Augustine, 'so that I forget my evils and embrace my one and only good, yourself?' God is a metaphorical hugger. And as a man in Christianity, the Lord certainly weeps, shouts, and prays. While dying on the cross, he asks: 'My God, My God, why hast Thou forsaken Me?' The Lord of Hosts has many moods.

But he does not shrug.

Perhaps he *can* shrug. After all, he is the almighty. 'With the word of His greatness has He assembled all that exists,' wrote Clement of Alexandria, 'and with a word He is able to overturn it again.' This is a huge, fearsome being. He creates seas and skies, punishes sinners, favours the pious. The psalms portray him as a strong defender and benefactor, and he is often worshipped this way: as a tough but fair sky-papa, shaking his strong right hand at enemies over his children's shaking shoulders. Sigmund Freud was wrong about Oedipus but right about this very domestic deification: 'At bottom God is nothing other than an exalted father.'

Theology is typically more careful. Yes, God's will is pure and perfect. As Thomas Aquinas argued, this follows from his basic existence: he is actuality itself; transcendent form, without any matter. Put another way, the Lord's power is limitless because it never meets anything beyond itself — there are literally no limits. Whatever he wants to be, just *is*; aspiration and achievement are one.

But God cannot will contradictions or evils: these are not possible, or not possible for him in his absolute goodness. Thinkers like the English Franciscan friar William of Ockham thought otherwise, arguing that God simply chooses to avoid paradoxes and vices: 'He is debtor to no one.' The mainstream theological consensus is with Aquinas, though. If it is possible for God, he can do it. If it is not possible in general or not possible for him as the almighty, he cannot. Writing a thousand years before Aquinas, Augustine was clear on this:

> he is rightly called 'all-powerful', although he has not the power to die, or to be mistaken. 'All-powerful' means that he does what he wills, and does not suffer what he does not will; otherwise he would be by no means all-powerful. It is just because he is all-powerful that there are some things he cannot do.

Judaic scholars kept largely to this cautious vision of God's power, as did authoritative Islamic theologians like al-Ghazali. To avoid a muddled, malicious God, a few restrictions are needed. He avoids folly and wrongdoing, but he remains the ultimate force in existence: the most high, against which all things are low.

This is why the Lord does not shrug: he is not like us. He is the antithesis of us.

Servility

Shrugging is for mortals. That is to say: for infirm, ignorant, and often indifferent beings.

A shrug can be as simple as lifted shoulders, or as sophisticated a pose of pursed lips, squinting eyes, raised palms. As a recurrent gesture, it has several movements and meanings but a broad common significance. While some believe it signifies lack of knowledge, it is better understood as a sign of distance or disengagement.

The shrug has a primal flinch to it, which was recognised many centuries ago by Quintilian. In his guide to public speaking, the first-century orator warned Latins against this gesture. 'Rarely is it becoming to shrug or hunch the shoulders,' he wrote, 'because this shortens the neck and produces a gesture of humiliation and servility.' Eighteenth-century English artist and critic William Hogarth thought it barbaric in dance: the savage opposite of formal French stiffness. When we shrug, we shrink back like animals avoiding danger. We show our empty hands, with nothing to threaten.

The point is not that we are simply a bundle of reflexes, that gestures are biological signals and nothing more. In fact, the shoulder shrug might develop after the raised palms — from mimicry, not instinct. The point is that we darn meaning with existing yarn. The shrug is a physiological spasm of fear, caution, or weakness that has become a psychological and societal symbol. This 'defensive crouching movement' typically means three things: helplessness, cluelessness, or heedlessness. In other words: *I cannot help*, *I do not know*, or *I do not care*.

Like laughter, the shrug introduces a gap between ourselves and the world, a void that affords us a little space from concern or responsibility. We might raise our hands to pray or beg, but we lift our shoulders when this fails.

'Jews'

Jews shrug.

And what are Jews? According to bigots, they are crafty cosmopolitans. Rootless and merciless, they love money and hate gentiles. They exploit manly labourers with their effete intellectual wiles; they count their shekels from the shadows. Philosopher and antisemite Martin Heidegger, from his diaries:

> One of the most secret forms of the *gigantic*, and perhaps the oldest, is the tenacious skillfulness in calculating, hustling, and intermingling through which the worldlessness of Jewry is grounded.

This Jew does not exist. Like Marlowe's Barabas, he is what Stephen Greenblatt called 'a fiction composed of the sleaziest materials in his culture'. This sick fantasy was invented by early followers of Christ, and it grew in power as the Church did. It opposes pious, honest Christians to a stiff-necked, sneaky enemy. Indeed, antisemitism is best defined by its illusions, falsely believing that actual Jews are these 'Jews'.

There is no arguing with this lie, and this is the point: it provides bigots with an easy selfhood. They need suffer no ambiguity or ambivalence in themselves; they are simply virtuous gentiles in contrast to these Hebrew monsters. In this, the ideology offers antisemites what Jean-Paul Sartre called 'the durability of a stone'. While this hatred of Jews has now been globalised beyond Christianity, the logic is the same. Modern antisemites stuff a puppet full of their own vices and jeer at it, feeling themselves more humbly virtuous as a consequence — and more simply, effortlessly real.

Fictitious Jews love to shrug, because they are the personification of distance or disengagement. They are seemingly subservient, yes — weak, clumsy, spindly. It makes sense for these hollow-chested, flat-footed cowards to cringe. But they are also the ultimate Other. They do not commit to this soil or Volk; not to this language or law. They are characterised by their ironic mockery of all ordinary folk and their ordinary values.

Witness a postcard from New York, printed in the early twentieth century: 'Vy not?' asks a cartoon Ashkenazi immigrant. See his large hooked nose, thick red lips, hooded eyes, black curly hair — and all under a yellow bowler or derby. And see his big shrug: arms and hands akimbo, an absurd caricature. The Jew will not give you an honest answer, will not face you, man to man. He will simply raise his shoulders and palms, turning your question against you. Why not?

Supposedly, the shrug of the stereotypical Jew is proof that he is a cunning, nihilistic, sneering liar. And *this* is the lie: that such a villain exists.

What is the truth? The 'Jew' is what bigots hate in themselves; he is their own weakness, ignorance, and indifference personified. This is why he shrugs.

Jews

And yet, Jews shrug. We do.

Consider Jewish author Saul Bellow's partly autobiographical character Herzog, thinking of his father's death and crumbling bones — the infinite, indifferent cosmos going from emptiness to emptiness. Then he gives 'one of his Jewish shrugs', whispering to himself, 'Be that as it may.' In *The American Jewess*, a well-to-do correspondent writes about a poor child in London's East End: the little olive-seller gives 'a truly Jewish shrug of her small shoulders' when her goods are judged poorly. Comedian Joan Rivers — born Joan Alexandra Molinsky — does not simply shrug, she gives 'the Jewish shrug'. And so on.

Does such a gesture exist? If Jews shrug Jewishly, two tendencies stand out.

To begin, Jews are bookish. This is not a trope of hunched nebbishes, stumbling at sport. And not all Jews were literate. This is a cultural bent: textuality has been vital for Jews as Jews. Everyone was supposed to hear God's laws read aloud, even foreigners: 'men and women, and children, and thy stranger that is within thy gates'. And every man was supposed to study the Torah. (Another patriarchy.) Yes, there were oral traditions: generations of spoken judgements, tales, arguments. But many of these were transcribed and edited too — so centuries of conflict entered the canon in the Talmud alongside the Torah. Especially after Rome smashed Jerusalem's temple in the first century, these holy books became portable homelands. And in these lands, Jews sought guides. A new ideal of piety arose alongside the priest and prophet: the scholar.

Enter rabbis. Like theologians, these masters are fiends for interpretation, but they (thankfully) lack a Vatican to sort orthodoxy from heterodoxy, piety from heresy. In Judaism, there are no papal bulls, no universal creeds. There are customs and rites, but no official dogma. The same texts are not read in the same ways. And because of this, Jews are familiar with disputes that continue without conclusion — or conclude without ultimate finality. This gives rise to what scholar Michael Fishbane calls 'a culture of exegetical intensity and debate, of conflicts and contradictions'. This need not be furious or malicious — it can be done with friendliness and goodwill.

Obviously Jewish institutions are not anarchic squats.

There can still be exclusions and excommunications, spats and bans. A noted Talmudic scholar in his youth, the philosopher Spinoza was famously cast out from the Amsterdam community for his ideas. Yet he kept his rabbinical outlook. 'Cast away this deadly superstition,' he told a pupil who became a Catholic, 'acknowledge the reason which God has given you.'

Rabbis are even depicted arguing with God himself. In one famous passage of the Talmud, Rabbi Eliezer judges that a new oven is ritually pure. His colleagues naysay this. To prove himself, Eliezer does not continue with argument. Instead, he lets divine power prosecute his case. If he is right, he says, the carob tree will move, the stream will change its flow, the walls will lean in — and these things all happen magically. But the others ask: what do trees, streams, or walls have to do with their judgements? The Lord then tells the rabbis that Eliezer is right. Still, the others will not have it: what do God's words have to do with their judgements? They quote Deuteronomy: 'It is not in heaven.' The law is the law, and it is in *their* hands, not up in the sky. God laughs: 'My children have outvoted Me, My children have outvoted Me!'

This is partly how Jews shrug: with the raised shoulders and palms of those who live with doubt. For all our backbone and strut, we know our knowledge is petty. The Talmudic rabbis were victorious over the Lord, but they still had one another to war with. For every 'yes', there is a 'but'; for every 'ah ha', a 'nu'. Well? And? So?

Jews are also outsiders. Our identity begins with stories of exile, and we have been shunned and abused for many lifetimes. This is not the whole of Jewish existence, and living near other Jews can ease the anxiety of life among Christians. Jewish fear can also be manipulated for political ends, disguising brutality as vulnerability and hostility as victimhood. Yet the dread itself is understandable, arising from a long history of aggression and oppression. No Jew who has even a nodding familiarity with this legacy can pretend they are perfectly safe. We remember what Magda Teter calls 'a heritage of social tolerance for killing Jews'. We know how quickly assimilation gives way to antagonism. 'There is something in the historical Jewish experience of persecution,' writes poet Richard Fein, 'that instructs the Jew to be prepared to run, carrying with him only what he possesses in his skull.'

Because of this, Jews often lack the cosmic tranquility that comes with belonging — the feeling that reality simply is what it is. We always live in interesting times.

So, Jews are familiar with ambiguity: fervently committed to the here and now, and fervently aware that the universe does not answer to us. We feel the necessity of our lives alongside their absolute contingency. In short, we know absurdity.

And this is why we shrug: other than laughing, what else can we do?

Jews have no unique relationship to scepticism and duality. This is yet another false Jewish monopoly. We are all heirs to this legacy — if we are brave (or wretched) enough to recognise it. As enlightened human beings, we are free to know our own lack of freedom, intelligent enough to know how much of the world and ourselves is thoughtless, aware of our smallness in the universe, while also feeling ourselves the centre of this universe. Simone de Beauvoir put this neatly in *The Ethics of Ambiguity*, writing that each of us is a 'pure internality' that no power can overcome, yet also 'a thing crushed by the dark weight of other things'.

Like other outcasts and exiles, Jews have enjoyed fewer chances to deny this double existence. This does not make us good. It is no shortcut to virtue or even practicality. It merely pushes us to feel the ridiculousness of our reality — or it *should*.

The Abrahamic God is a consolation for this reality. A fantasy of eternal perfection, his being is everything that ours is not. He is a Lord of shruggers who himself will never shrug — and never needs to.

A god who shrugs

I have yet no need of gods. But if I were especially keen — perhaps melancholy, perhaps jubilant, perhaps mad — what kind of god or gods might I entertain?

Friedrich Nietzsche's hero Zarathustra famously said that his deity would dance: a spirit of nimbleness and lightness, existing with cheer. This was also Nietzsche's vision of philosophy itself.

(The Lord dances occasionally. He spins with joy as the Father, and shakes a leg at Passover as the Son — apocryphally, at least. But dancing is not his hallmark.)

Not long after Nietzsche died, H.P. Lovecraft wrote of a cosmic elder god, sleeping under the ocean: a spirit of mad abandon. When Cthulhu wakes, he will encourage frenzied, ecstatic cruelty. This is a god who tortures.

(The Lord tortures Eve, Job, and many others. But torture is not his hallmark.)

I am perhaps too jaded for these divinities. I like to imagine a god who shrugs. Confronted by mortals

— stubborn, petty, foolhardy, capricious, gulled — my divinity wants to distance or disengage themselves from us.

This is no biblical Lord, no ghost of eternal perfection. The Abrahamic God is defined by what he needs: nothing. As Aristotle noted, such a being does not even need friends.

My god is antithetical to this, shrugging because they need us.

Perhaps they are like Nikos Kazantzakis' savage divinity: a spirit of ceaseless destruction and creation, but who requires our flesh to be realised. 'Our God is not almighty, he is not all-holy,' the Greek author wrote, 'he is not certain that he will conquer, he is not certain that he will be conquered.' Perhaps they are like Alfred North Whitehead's more genteel god: the lure for our creative energies, and the net that catches and keeps what we create. 'God is *in* the world, or nowhere,' he told a friend, 'creating continually in us and around us.'

Whatever their genius or brawn, this deity of mine cannot achieve their ideals alone. Because they are processes or principles, not beings of blood and bone, they can goad or invite — but they cannot *do*. They need us in the filth of things, soiling our hands.

Alas.

We will fumble. In ways petty and grand, we fail ourselves and one other — and no god of mine can remedy this. They might actually worsen our spirits by confronting us constantly with our own frailty. Like pure Prince Myshkin in *The Idiot*, their excellence might leave us embittered, not encouraged.

My god cannot overcome any of this. Knowing this weakness, they will ultimately do exactly as I do: lift their shoulders and palms.

Why? Because perfection is a fantasy — sometimes an orienting constellation amid the muck, but just as often a sightless lurch or flinch away from it. In politics and morality, there are no simple means to equally simple ends. Even with vast knowledge and goodwill, we will err. And to continue, we must tolerate this in one another. This is not a licence to lie and cheat, not a certificate of nihilism. We must make and honour our promises. But when we fail — and we will, again and again and again — we have to spare one another from merciless judgement. This allows us to try again. And again. And again.

This is my modest cult: deity and mortals, eternally shrugging at one another with forgiveness.

Ply, Pliable, Pliant

Drawn in black chalk, the dancer is squatting: gastrocnemius and adductor muscles standing out against her otherwise smooth lines. There is a soft obliqueness to her, a suggestion of easy diagonals, from shoulders, to arms, to thighs.

These give an impression of downward movement, but stilled: the dancer is neither collapsing nor paralysed, neither fast nor fastened. Instead, she is easing herself down, allowing gravity to assist but not acquire her. I look for strain and find none — no bulging eyes, gritted teeth, or signs of panting. In fact, she is drawn with her eyes and mouth shut: each just a short curved or flat line in her oval face. Despite her toes being turned out — the levers to her knees and hips' hinges — she is calm.

The dancer in Edgar Degas' *Plié in Second Position at the Barre* performed this squat well over a century ago, and the gesture was already antique when she learned it as a girl in the Paris Opéra. Yet to anyone glancingly familiar with European arts, she is no exotic mystery. Even without her tutu and bodice, the dancer is recognisable as a ballerina. Her pose has kept its signature form if not its special significance.

So, we need not know ballet to know Degas' dancer is balletic. She is performing perhaps the most basic of all classical positions, which Imperial Russian educator Agrippina Vaganova described as 'inherent in all dance'.

Mastering herself, she is surrendering to an ideal: the plié.

Squat

The plié is not an ordinary squat, but it is a squat nonetheless. Yes, the arse is tucked in, not jutting; the right and left toes are aloof to one another, while the heels are intimate; the arms are often raised or holding the barre rather than supporting a weighted rack. But the basic movement is the same: the legs bend, but not the back. And it is everywhere. 'Whether you've danced once or a thousand times,' writes dancer and artistic director David Hallberg, 'it is the plié that begins your day.'

From the Latin for 'fold', whence we have 'ply', 'pliable', and 'pliant', the plié is a conditioning exercise. It strengthens muscles, stretches ligaments; it challenges coordination and balance. This is why Romantic air spirit Marie Taglioni exercised for two hours before bed every night — including a grand plié so low that she touched her hands to the floor. This squat is a physical discipline that encourages some physiques and not others.

In this, we might say that the chief meaning of the plié is perseverance. Plato called perseverance 'our ability to remain calm and endure', though he wrongly saw it as a manly virtue. This excellence allows us to press on, despite psychological or physical pain. Ballerinas are certainly no strangers to suffering: torn-off toenails, flayed heels, and a miscellany of strains and breaks. Jenifer Ringer, principal dancer with the New York City Ballet: 'I became good friends with the ice bucket.'

But the plié is more than physical training. As a feature of every classical performance, it is both preparation for dance and also dance itself. Russian critic Akim Volynsky described the plié as the earth to the vault's sky, the 'plantlike and pliant' ground to the soaring ballon. When the performers jump, they begin and end with a plié. It can be this descent that makes the ascent seem so soaring. George Balanchine, the Georgian-born master of American ballet, told his dancers that Vaslav Nijinsky's secret was not his take-off but his landing: its stability suggested a lofty ease. In fact, the plié can be a dance all of its own. In Béjart's choreography for Ravel's *Boléro*, Maya Plisetskaya did hundreds of 'springy squats' between the melodies. They were themselves part of his sensuous, sensual vision.

No one thing

The plié's ubiquity makes its meaning supple.

In Balanchine's *Nutcracker*, it is a waltzing flower's carefree exuberance; in *Swan Lake*, Odile's slow seduction; in *The Sleeping Beauty*, Aurora's naive glee before her fall — and this is only from Russian fin de siècle classical ballets. It might also be a Victorian lady's prudish judgement in Antony Tudor's *Pillar of Fire*, or the exquisitely precise drama of Balanchine's *Agon*. And so on. The plié has no single meaning, since it is the base of so much meaningful dance: the foundation, which allows for the rising architectures.

Dance itself is no one thing. It is best understood as another kind of language — and language is not simply true or false statements. It is more like a miscellany of games with miscellaneous rules. It is something we play together, yes — but also something we play variously. Likewise, dance can be performed as celebration or memorial, metaphorical suggestion or literal pantomime, confession or accusation. It does not merely communicate different things — it communicates these *differently*.

So, classical ballet is only one tradition within dance. And even within this history there are conflicting ideas of beauty — and some reject beauty altogether as the one ideal. There are ballets of dramatic longing, like Taglioni's *La Sylphide*; of stark brutality, like MacMillan's *The Invitation*; of comedic whimsy, like Ashton's *The Dream*. Because of this, the plié can never signify just one thing: it shifts with its milieu. Blaise Pascal, writing while Louis XIV was the king of dance:

> How many natures lie in human nature! How many occupations! How fortuitously in the ordinary way each of us takes up the one that he has heard others praise. A well-turned heel.

Is the plié empty, then? An exotic sack, into which any significance is stuffed?

Verticality

The ballet squat is certainly pliable, literally and figuratively. But it has its own domain of genius, which began half a millennia ago: verticality.

What became classical ballet arose in sixteenth-century France, as the Florentine queen Catherine de' Medici brought dance to the court of Henry II. This Renaissance art was supposed to introduce divine mathematical harmonies into profane flesh. Like Plato, many nobles believed this was morally educational. In their Neoplatonic cosmos, matter was feral stuff, in need of taming by mind. By dancing these higher forms, kings and courtiers alike were making themselves more virtuous.

In the next century, dance continued to be a courtly pursuit. In fact, it became *the* art of Louis XIV, the Sun King: a talented, passionate dancer. But in this regime, la danse noble was no longer simply an edifying movement. Instead, it was a way to revere and ritualise the state hierarchy. The body was political. As always, the aristocracy was identified with certain poses and gaits; certain positions in a room, or beside one another. Nobles' artworks celebrated them in dance poses, with one court portrait having the Sun King himself in fourth position, left foot turned neatly in buckled heels. Ballet was vital to their felt superiority.

In this symbolic universe, the 'high' in highborn was no dead metaphor. To be beneath someone in birth and favour was literally to be under them, to have a more stooped carriage, to be bent by labour and worry. Just as importantly, it was to revere more humbly — and this is the very origin of the plié. To show courtesy, whence we have 'curtsy', was to lower oneself. 'The greater the person bowed to,' writes dancer and historian Jennifer Homans, 'the deeper the bend of the knees.'

Like fencing, ballet eventually became professionalised: the province of bourgeois masters and performers. The centre of dance performance moved from Versailles to the Paris Opéra, and it became more public than private spectacle. But the ideal of noble grace and power continued, as paid teachers taught dance, swordplay, and riding to the children of the highborn. Through ballet and its purported virtues, the middle classes gained royal privileges or coin — and the royals gained their 'natural' grace. Here, to be an upright gentleman was to be upright: 'the vertical, balanced stance of the dancer'.

The Enlightenment and French Revolution encouraged dance of greater simplicity and supposed honesty. Some thought gesture was more primal and immediate, a way to avoid the pomp and fakery of other arts. The philosopher Jean-Jacques Rousseau even wrote a version of *Pygmalion* that was as much pantomime as opera, the actors miming to music. This style did not last, but another consequence of the Gallic civil war did: Napoleon's absolutism. In his reign, ballet was standardised, part of an enormous bureaucracy. In this, it became something more familiar to us today, what Homans describes as 'the first outlines of ballet as a modern discipline'.

While France kept its pomp and hierarchies, ballet

ceased to be an aristocratic classroom. Bodies were no longer elite or common by birth: they were simply well or poorly trained. Dance became a distinct repertoire, not a class privilege. And instead of regal austerity, a new style was championed: the athletic, gymnastic dance of common-born Auguste Vestris. After years of gruelling training, virtuosi like him sported with gravity. One critic wrote: '[he] executes such perilous leaps and bounds, with such vigor, that his head is elevated above all the other dancers.' They called him the 'god of the dance': height meant divinity.

Ecce ballerina

But these deities died. This was not because their virtuosity was snubbed, but because men were no longer the stars. The bourgeois French wrung their hands about weak masculinity. They were worried that dance was effete, that a love of beautiful theatricality went hand in glove with a hatred of solid middle-class virtue. Prancing dandies like Vestris were too much to tolerate on the stage. Exit ballerino. Enter ballerina.

What we know as classical ballet arose from this new era: seemingly weightless fairies, sylphs, princesses. Partly a reaction against capitalist materialism, Romantic ballet took over. One of the stars was Marie Taglioni, who took Vestris' tough physicality and put it to the service of spiritual yearning. Physical height as spiritualised transcendence. Vestris also trained dancers including Marius Petipa, who gave French Romanticism a precise Russian magnitude. These works are still standards today: *The Sleeping Beauty*, *The Nutcracker*, and of course *Swan Lake*. (When Taylor Swift wants to best highlight her own clumsy, zany authenticity, it is the swan's tutu and bodice she dons.)

Despite profound political, moral, and aesthetic shifts, ballets from sixteenth-century France to nineteenth-century Russia all toyed with depth and height. There was always the illusion that, at their most glorious, dancers were not ordinary animals but divine beings with tireless muscles and light bones. And they eventually seemed to have no muscles and bones whatsoever — they were mist or light or flowers. This was partly the invention of the proscenium: the stage that turned the courtly dance into a tableau. Here, verticality became more important than the court's horizontal geometries. But it was also that original aristocratic ideal, which saw the dancer as higher than the rest — physically, morally, metaphysically.

And to raise herself, the ballerina must first become low. Master Pierre Rameau, with a bold phrase from the eighteenth century: 'Dancing is no more than to know how to sink and rise properly.' This cannot be done jerkily or shudderingly. It must be pure grace: great difficulty without the slightest superfluity.

In this, Degas' dancer is practising humility of a stripe, allowing herself to be disciplined by the tradition. Yet this is what allows her to gain power and grace.

In the plié, the ballerina is telling us this: *I bow to artistic necessity, but not to gravity.*

Springs, pivots, levers

So, each dancer is the heir to a legacy of transcendence. Yet this bequest is fleshy.

Ballet is a manual art, with the dancer's physique shaped daily by teachers and choreographers. For centuries, these performances were rarely recorded in paper and ink. Instead, they were written in the dancers' bodies, *as* the dancers' bodies. While the aesthetic values were sometimes mediated by painting and statuary, the performers themselves had a more immediate schooling: a pedagogy of touch and close sight. The plié of Degas' dancer was literally handed on from master to pupil, master to pupil, over hundreds of years.

There were variations: perhaps a more turned-out foot, a higher arm. And dance was often as theoretical as practical, illuminated by abstract concepts of world and self. Even Balanchine's casual 'just do the steps' was a profession of faith: do your modest job, and trust that the universe will take care of itself. But as a practice for performers, ballet was typically an intimate affair.

And it still is. There are new notations and media, new ways of keeping swift, subtle movements from being annihilated by time. Yet ballet still needs older hands on younger arms, still needs to nudge a wrist here, a foot there, and the back just so. Children might first witness ballet from afar, in the darkened auditorium. But to become dancers, they must go behind the proscenium, where their physiques and physicalities will become problems. There, the distance they once had from the stage will open up *within* them: between their consciousnesses and their bodies; between themselves as subjects and objects. They will become a collection of springs, pivots, levers — to be taken apart, put back together, then hidden behind the well-crafted case of beauty and ease. Ballerina and author Renée K. Nicholson: 'My body was always a work in progress.'

Little rats

In this way, Degas' dancer literally incorporated an ideal. But whose ideal?

Certainly not hers. Ballet is an intimate art, but its workshops are not built and run on reveries. They are staffed by professionals who compose, choreograph, and clothe. Companies have directors and accountants, theatres have ushers and cleaners. All this must be paid for, if only by the state. And alongside coin, there is symbolic capital: the currency of physicality, gained only through disciplined devotion to the field. You can change ballet only by becoming it fully, by replicating what it replicated in you. Ultimately, only a handful decide on who dances and what they dance. This is as true now as it was in aristocratic Paris, imperial Saint Petersburg, or capitalist New York.

Most masters of ballet have been men. And women are taught to break and bruise themselves in service of men's fantasies: the airy sylph, the ethereal princess. Though their bodies howl, they learn not to listen, learn to mute their own calls for salve or sympathy.

When women took over in the footlights, men still ruled behind the stage. Think of the Paris Opéra in the second half of the nineteenth century. Many of the 'little rats' who worked there were not high bourgeois girls with economic and social capital — that is, with coin and esteem. They were poor and poorly educated. Ballet was a way to gain a trade, and perhaps a patron.

Having paid well for the privilege, wealthy members were allowed to roam in search of exoticised, eroticised youth. On stage, the girls were otherworldly maidens from the Orient or Indias; in the foyer de la danse, they were affordable companions. This reputation continued for generations. French-born Hollywood dancer Leslie Caron told her family she wanted to be a professional dancer. A man of the previous century, her grandfather was aghast: 'Margaret! Do you want your daughter to be a whore?'

And how did Edgar Degas get his sketchpad and chalks backstage? He too was a bourgeois — not rich, but far wealthier than les petits rats. And he knew it. He was also far more connected. His friends invited him to watch the dancers until he was a member of the Opéra himself. He said he enjoyed stripping the girls of their coquetry. This was less about sadistic misogyny, and more about painterly realism: revealing the flesh-and-blood beasts behind the stage lights, tulle, and make-up. He drew them in their private moments, or had them in painful poses for hours. 'For me, the essential thing is to express nature in all its aspects and motion with the utmost precision,' he said, 'to accentuate bone and muscle and the compact firmness of flesh.'

The hierarchy here was not simply artistic. Think of the model in Degas' now-famous sculpture *Little Dancer Aged Fourteen*. Marie van Goethem was the child of a laundress, a profession caricatured as morally filthy for all its cleanliness. 'It cannot be said,' wrote one popular historian, 'that their souls are as immaculate as the linen they iron.' In short, they were *available*. Degas drew the childlike adolescent nude in fourth position, one of many works that illustrated these unclothed, unguarded girls from multiple views. Again. Again. Again. He was an artist, yes. But he was also a brutal anatomist of sorts, trying to capture these caged and flayed animals on paper.

Degas' interest was not lewd, however much

his buyers' might have been. His abiding mood was amazement. Robert Hughes put this well: 'His libido and curiosity were channeled through his eyes.' The painter cared profoundly for music and ballet and devoted himself piously to the study of gesture and perspective. As a draftsman, he was patient and studious. As a painter, he was revelatory in his honesty. 'People call me the painter of dancing girls,' he told art dealer Ambroise Vollard. 'It has never occurred to them that my chief interest in dancers lies in rendering movement and painting pretty clothes.'

Still, enthusiasm and talent cannot overcome power. Degas was a studio labourer painting stage labourers, but he did so as a middle-class man in an age built for middle-class men.

Today, women in ballet remain poorer in cash and sway. They are less likely to run and choreograph the companies, less likely to be paid fairly. And the standard ballet story is typically about wispy damsels or tragic exotics, rather than whole, free beings. Female bodies, male stories. And those who are neither gender or both? Ballet rarely stretches.

Yes, professional ballet is no longer stigmatised as a posh knocking-shop, and the amateur art offers more playful freedom than misogynistic harm. But classical dance cannot deny its nineteenth-century Gallic legacy: bared female bodies, literally and figuratively manipulated by dressed men.

With her plié, Degas' dancer bowed to form — but also to patriarchy.

Rising

The plié symbolises a neat duality: between the ease of the spectacle and the effort needed to perform it. What looks like ethereal flight involves strained calves, torn toenails — and often twisting guts.

This is part of ballet's great aesthetic conceit. It suggests the transcendent, the eternal, the universal — it has a glimmer of divinity to it. In this vision, the art is not merely one style of dance from Europe, not merely another ethnic play. Instead, it is a metaphysical essence. Choreographer William Forsyth: 'You cannot do arabesque — arabesque exists as an idea.' Here, classical dance does not create techniques, so much as discover them: like Plato's Forms, glimpsed before being born again.

Of course, the techniques are not simply in 'that place beyond the heavens,' as Plato put it. They are made up by sweaty, stumbling mortals. And then they are *made*: practice after practice, show after show. It takes toil to make toil look simple and straightforward.

And so it is with patriarchy. A tireless performance of national laws and personal habits, of intimate prizes and intimate punishments, of twee fantasies and grim facts — it takes toil to make toil look simple and straightforward. Domination becomes the everlasting way of things. Common if not comfortable.

This is the very definition of ideology: pretending the contingent is necessary, the artificial is god-given or organic. Each of us becomes an *obvious* something for one another and ourselves. This is not just about beliefs, but also about how we live. Little girls are given a checklist: these skirts in only these colours (if colour is allowed), this way of swinging the hips (if hips are allowed), those ways of biting food (if food is allowed). These practices change by era and ethnicity and class, but they are still seen as changeless. Of course things are this way — they were supposed to be this way all along. How much dogma there is in the 'natural'.

Simone de Beauvoir famously quipped that a woman is made, not simply born. And how carefully and perhaps cruelly Degas' dancer was made. She was drawn squatting so beautifully — but it was the artist who rose and kept rising.

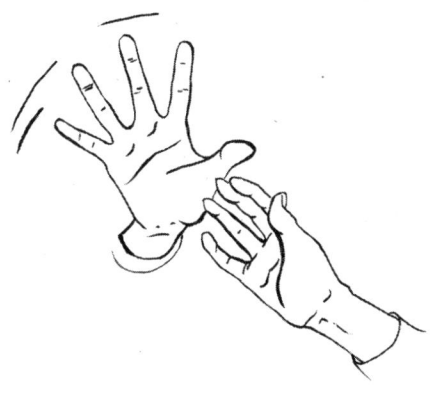

Unclean, Undead

Wearing a grey blazer, the famous scholar has something tucked under his arm. Perhaps a leather document case. Perhaps a manila folder. I cannot remember this detail, because what the professor holds is trivial to me. What matters are his free fingers.

Walking into the toilets where I stand, he steps up to the urinal. Papers still beneath his elbow and armpit, he sprays the urinal. Then the hand that guided his cock zips him up, pushes the button, and swings to-and-fro as he leaves the white-tiled room.

He does not pause. He pisses, flushes, walks away.

Not long after, I am introduced to this intellectual — the junior to the senior, the naïf to the well established. We loiter near the buffet. Smiling with goodwill, he offers his hand to me. It is *that* hand, which so recently touched his wet penis, the greasy cistern, and the smudged door handle; that hand that was never washed.

He looks at me, his grey hair high and wide. 'Nice to finally meet you.'

I look at his hand. I greet him with a nod. No handshake. Just a nod.

Clasping

What am I forsaking here? A common world of fraternity.

The handshake is an ancient rite — esteemed if not sacrosanct. It perhaps began as way to avoid violence: you showed your empty palm, with neither knife nor cudgel. You shook it; nothing sharp or heavy fell from your sleeve.

Often described as a gesture of trust, this is better understood as one of safety. Trust requires moral steadfastness: someone doing the right thing by you *because* it is the right thing, rather than because they are afraid, sneaky, or simply prudent. Whereas the most basic handshake just guarantees a brief lack of danger. Enemies can clasp one another's palms or wrists without a drop of trustworthiness between them.

Witness the ancient Roman legend of the Sabines: fathers and husbands are about to slaughter one another, while their daughters and wives plead for peace. The menfolk listen. 'The weapons and the passions of the warriors fall,' wrote Ovid, 'and laying their swords aside, fathers-in-law and sons-in-law grasp each other's hands.' The men are not friends here. They are not even cautious allies. In their handshake, they have achieved a pledge of truce and little more.

Yet even in classical antiquity, the handshake was already more than this promise of security. These doubled hands signified parting and arriving, farewell and welcome — often for intimates, and often in death. In the Roman empire, it was also an official emblem of concordia: harmony in marriage, and the patron goddess of the same.

Over the centuries, the handshake was familiar enough to Western Europeans, though its meanings changed. After the Renaissance, it was chiefly avoided by the aristocracies. They favoured gestures of rank like the bow, the curtsy, the raised hat. Even in the eighteenth century, British gentleman did not typically shake hands with strangers — touch suggested too much amity. Etiquette from afar was better.

During the Regency era, these customs became curt: a nod, a bob, a quick doff. It was not until well into the nineteenth century that the handshake became a common rite of fraternity — first in Britain, then in the Netherlands, then eventually in France. Skin to skin, men recognised one another's equality. And it was typically men who clasped palms, though not always. See Harriet Smith in Austen's *Emma*, delighted that the rich girl took her hand:

> Miss Woodhouse was so great a personage in Highbury, that the prospect of the introduction had given as much panic as pleasure; but the humble, grateful little girl went off with highly gratified feelings, delighted with the affability with which Miss Woodhouse had treated her all the evening, and actually shaken hands with her at last!

Nowadays, the handshake is a well-known ritual of mutual acknowledgement. It offers and asks for the favour of rapport. Aside from mass ceremonies, this begins or ends moments of regard, punctuates our sociability. It is not overly intimate, but it suggests solidarity and respect.

This is especially so in business. Even through plague times, men like to touch one another's hands, to come together as confident, capable individuals and make deals. The ritual is unsanitary and unnecessary, spreading pathogens while being easily replaced with other greetings. But men want to grip and tug and shake. It is how they recognise one another as autonomous, rational beings. 'If two individuals cannot coordinate their efforts to shake hands with one another,' writes anthropologist Deborah Schiffrin, 'one might suspect that in sustaining a relationship they would be even less able.'

By snubbing the professor, I am refusing this relationship and rejecting him — there will be no rapport. This is a professional risk, but I prefer it to the medical risk of *that* hand. The lack of one gesture means the lack of another: no washing, no shake. For me, the celebrated scholar has already left the common world of acknowledgement.

Put another way, he has failed the most basic, primeval requirement for the rite: he is dangerous. Or, more correctly: polluted.

Pollution

My latrine companion has touched at least three knobs: the cistern, the door, and his own. All of these can host pathogens, and hands are good at spreading them.

While handwashing is complicated to institutionalise, it is simple, quick, and relatively cheap. The professor did not bother — and so he is straightforwardly dirty.

He is dirty in another important sense, though. This is because dirt concerns our most basic notions of existence. We all have a sense of what belongs together or apart — or who. We divide the world into fundamental categories that cannot be transgressed without offence, fear, loathing, or ridicule. Anthropologist Mary Douglas argued that our symbols of dirt arise from these categories. When we part what is typically joined together or join what is typically parted — then we have dirt. It 'offends against order', as Douglas put it. At its simplest, dirt is what philosopher and psychologist William James called 'matter out of place'. And what defines this place? Chiefly culture.

For ancient Israelites, priests had to cleanse themselves regularly: 'When they go into the tent of meeting, or when they come near the altar to minister, to burn a food offering to the Lord, they shall wash with water, so that they may not die.' But there was no cleansing heathens, who were morally filthy simply by living without God. In the centuries after the Second Temple was built in Jerusalem, ordinary Jews took up their own purity rites. For some, this was as much a social as a religious distinction. Against traditional priestly authority and rights, the sect of Pharisees sought to set themselves apart. So they believed everyone had to wash their hands before eating, not just priests.

Jesus continued many Jewish customs, but he himself was seen as a purifying power. He could not make a heathen clean, but he could scrub away ritual filth. He touched lepers and blood because such things were cleansed by his holy fingers. The scriptures also have Christ arguing against the Pharisees on cleanliness. 'Whatsoever thing from without entereth into the man, it cannot defile him,' he said, 'that which cometh out of the man, that defileth the man.' So menstruation and ejaculation were polluting because they came from people, but so was vice. Lying, arrogance, fornication. For Jesus, there was no need to bathe hands before meals — the soul itself needed catharsis.

The hands of Sunni Muslims must be clean before praying or touching the scriptures. This is not because Allah or the Qur'an can be polluted. Divinity is beyond filth. Instead, the Muslim's consciousness ought to be turned away from dross, and the washing rites are meant to accomplish this. Indeed, the purest Muslim is he who can recite the holy passages without reading a line — his mind is without stain. While Muslims are ethically clean by default, infidels are not: they are tainted because they do not submit to Allah. Yet even this depends on the community involved, as Christians and Jews were allowed the mosques of cosmopolitan trading cities. The dirt of unbelief is unstable.

For Shaivites of India, only Shiva can worship Shiva. That is, it takes a divine being to properly recognise and celebrate a divine being. So these priests must become godly through ablution. This is less about keeping the deities free from grime — again, they are spiritually spotless — and more about showing esteem and cultivating a pious mood. Caste and cleanness are certainly related here, as Pariahs were thought to be contagious. The touch of the lowest supposedly left the highest vulnerable to sickness and demonic possession. And even now, few Dalits are priests. Yet these hierarchies are by no means identical: elite Brahmins are not those of greatest religious purity. Piety is its own kind of sovereignty.

In Imperial China, heaven or nature was clear and bright, whereas vice and illness were cloudy, dim. Much was made of women's oozings and drippings, which threatened men's health. Even the gods themselves were in danger from this. (Semen was life-giving. Of course.) These ideas worked between individuals, but also within the Confucian state. The job of virtuous rulers was to keep the good energies flowing freely, to keep the community from becoming stagnant. While Daoists famously raged against Confucianism, they too cleaved to clarity. Their rituals — washing, chants, movements — cleaned consciousness for fresh revelation to pour in. That is to say, they allowed the already-pure truth of things to enter the now-pure mind.

In each of these communities, muck was (and is) more than just soil or crap. It depended upon concepts of self, other, world; of neighbours and strangers; of states of mind and what they included or excluded.

So, ideas of dirtiness and cleanliness are ontological. They help to make sense of the universe. Or rather, universes. Each society has its own design instructions: how things fit together, and when they ought not to. These are not quite moral ideas, yet they are often felt beneath or alongside concepts of good and evil, virtue or duty. Many believe that transgressors will suffer, and this will not happen through mere custom or law. 'This anonymous wrath, this faceless violence of Retribution,' wrote Paul Ricoeur, 'is inscribed in the human world in letters of suffering.' The very way of things will hurt the polluted, will give them sickness or grief.

For good or ill, these rites help to keep people together, and often become stricter when they are threatened. The more 'they' attack 'us', the more fastidiously each of us must defend ourselves with exacting sanitation: purging the filth.

Yes, the faithful are not theologians or philosophers — we ought not falsify life by neatening it academically. (Scholarly purity: the intellectual's fear of conceptual mess.) But it is vital to recognise the cultures behind our ideas of dirt. Cleanliness is not some universal and eternal essence, some fact of biology or divine command.

Purity is a creative achievement. We build worlds together, then we try to keep them neat.

Damned spot

But I am not an Aaronite priest entering the temple or a Pharisee haranguing Christ; not a Sunni Muslim before al-Ka'aba or a Shaivite libating the lingam; not a Confucian seeking justice or a Daoist longevity. Why do I care about washed hands?

Intellectually and ethically, this is because of public health. Dirty hands are literally sickening.

But more viscerally, it is because I am a mortal: carnal, vulnerable, fleeting. The sense of pollution arises from my physical existence itself, from what it feels like to be mired in bright blood, sour bile, sticky shit, oozing semen. Things inside are suddenly outside; things that are yours are suddenly on or in me. Categories are warped or broken entirely. Purity customs always make sense within a given society, but the basic metaphor is part of our common legacy of flesh. This is why primal loathing works better to encourage handwashing than microbiological facts. If you want people lathering and rinsing their palms, show them vile things first. Disgust trumps documentation.

Think of the lasting power of these themes in drama. While written in Christian England during the Renaissance, Shakespeare has been performed in Hebrew, Greek, Arabic, Hindi, Chinese. ('Stoop, then, and wash. How many ages hence / Shall this our lofty scene be acted over / In states unborn and accents yet unknown!') The Bard's plays work dramatically over distance, temporal and spatial. Over four centuries since *Macbeth* was first performed, we do not need to be told why the Lady is scrubbing spots from her spotless hands. We understand immediately that she is hallucinating her guilt. In her madness, she is quite sane in this. Complicit in the murder of the king in her home, she has sinned doubly: committing regicide as a vassal and killing a guest as an 'honour'd hostess'. The blood on her hands is figurative but quite real.

Yes, this is more moral than ritual purity. But the second continues in the first, giving our ethical systems their flinch and shudder. Like the Jacobeans who gasped or hooted at the lady's ravings, we know that transgressions seem to stain us, and that these stains point back to the transgressions. ('[U]nnatural deeds / Do breed unnatural troubles: infected minds / To their deaf pillows will discharge their secrets.') Evil is a mark of sorts, something foul that seeps and spreads.

In this light, when I wash my hands I am doing more than ridding myself of pathogens. I am also ridding myself of anxiety. Blame runs down the plughole, often along with guilt or shame. Soaping and scrubbing, I am passing symbolically between spaces and states — urinal to hall, excretion to conversation, unclean to unspoiled. I am transformed and saying to myself: *the cosmos is now as it ought to be*. However briefly, I have introduced a little order into the chaos.

And the important academic with his tranche of important texts? He enters and exits the toilet doorway unchanged, unredeemed. Because of this, he sticks together categories that must stay apart: penis and polite company, toilet and office, piss and buffet. He is ritually filthy. While no bacteria or plasmodia are seen wriggling on his palms, he is obviously and primally polluted. The lowest of the low.

I can only nod to him from my fresh, clean heights. A lesser gesture for a lesser gesture.

Spoiled

What is this scholar to me? (And perhaps to you.) How should I describe this persona non grata?

It is important to be careful here. I am not sketching the professor's character or personality, much less his so-called 'inner life'. As Hume observed in the eighteenth century and Buddhists many centuries earlier, the self is not something I can observe. It is not an object 'out there' for a subject 'in here', not a thing among things.

Yet we are human beings, surrounded by human beings; we live in a world of other selves. This is why Heidegger introduced ideas like Mitsein, or being-with, to his basic conception of humanity. Even when we are alone, others are part of our existence. We learn to see through behaviours: to purposes and urges, concepts and passions, decisions and tendencies. We are gregarious beasts.

Because of this, we also have selves that are more public than private, more communal than personal. These are our social identities, which we hurl ahead of ourselves and catch from others. A swagger or a saunter? Business suit or tasselled pasties and a stare? Simple Anglo-Saxon words or Latinate jargon? And so on, into a million niceties of waking life. This is a performance of self, meant with neither cynicism nor mockery.

When someone fails on this stage, they gain stigma, what Erving Goffman called a 'spoiled' identity. Importantly, these expectations are rarely fair or even reasonable. They are often superficial, capricious, and smug. Still, they seem like cosmic laws. So we hide our stigma, withdraw to similar or sympathetic comrades, or find ways to make the normals more at ease. This is a social identity of stress, hesitance, wariness. A self of not quite right. But also observe the *kind* of category this is: it exists to catch those who fall through the usual categories. It is a part of the system that allows for the system's breakages, strains, gaps.

My portrait of the scholar is of this kind. I am describing his spoiled identity for me in that lavatory and hall. Put another way, I am answering this question: what do I stigmatise him *as*?

Monstrous dirt

Holding out that hand so politely, the professor is like a zombie to me. This is not because he is rotting, groaning, gnashing. Rather, it is because of his logic: incongruous, thoughtless, antisocial.

Zombies are horrifying partly because they combine categories that ought to stay separate. Living dead, edible brains, visible viscera. They are monstrously dirty in Mary Douglas' sense: matter in the wrong place.

They are also disturbing because they are solely beings of routine. Zombies cannot choose, let alone reflect on their choices. Wholly at the whim of their most basic urges, they are biological necessity without existential freedom. And we fear this contagion because we are already somewhat infected. Much of our physical and psychological life is wholly automatic, a matter of chemical reactions, reflexes, instincts, habits — what Nietzsche called 'a mighty commander' and 'unknown sage'. The German philosopher was quite right to laud the flesh, but without a little liberty there is no Nietzsche to do the lauding. Our automatisms are powerful, yet they are not enough for humanity.

Finally, zombies symbolise the loss of civilisation. When they arrive, much else leaves: roads, schools, moral qualms, perhaps hope. More importantly, they have order, but no *social* order. They are united by appetite and nothing more; they simply hunt the same prey. They neither communicate nor cooperate. They just sniff, shuffle, groan, bite.

This is what makes my skin crawl at the scholar's spoiled identity. He has become polluted, anthropologically — a conceptual muddle. Without the cultivated custom of handwashing, he suggests humanity without liberty. And he has withdrawn from the community, from the enterprise of mutual recognition.

Might he regret this stigma? Perhaps. Though our zombie is not alone. Its filth is common among men, who like to shake hands but not to clean them. In this, they are more likely to spread infections and illness with a winning smile, a welcoming palm. They are also happy to seek one another's company, making what Goffman calls a 'circle of lament'. Some feel righteous pride in their manly contagion, even during a pandemic.

Carried along by the horde, zombies do not pause before doors — they smash these then continue on their way.

Conscience

Must I always cleanse myself, then?

No. Sometimes I *ought* to stay marked, if only to show others — and to show others that I know. This is especially so with moral pollution. Here, hands without stain can lie. If their marks are caused by wrongdoing, scouring these away is doubly false: it erases evidence of my crime, but it also suggests a pure soul where none exists.

Think of Rome's prefect in Judea, as he judged Christ. As this story is told, Jesus felt no need to wash his hands before eating, no ritual pollution from within himself. And he was neither ashamed nor guilty — as God made flesh, he was virtuous. But Pontius Pilate? Consider his famous gesture: 'he took water, and washed his hands before the multitude, saying, I am innocent of the blood of this just person: see ye to it.' Pilate ruled with all Rome's legal and military authority, and he knew it. He condemned an innocent with this rule, and he knew it. And he was using a Jewish religious gesture to avoid blame for this: bathing those palms and fingers, like a priest before the sacrifice. (How like an occupier.)

This worked well enough. Yes, some Christians remembered him as a wicked suicide, cursed by demons and storms to be buried in the Tiber, then the Rhône, then a pit in Switzerland. But he was also praised as a martyr by theologians and sainted by two churches. It was not Pilate who killed the messiah, argued Origen in the third century — it was the Jews. Was the governor himself anguished or even regretful? The gospels tell us little about this provincial administrator, and they are sacred literature not psychological studies. But Pilate seemingly lived a quiet life after his return to Rome.

The Romans were not without conscience, of course. It was common in their Stoic philosophy to see conscience as divine rationality. Seneca, to his friend Lucilius: 'God is near you, is with you, is inside of you ... a divine spirit, which guards us and watches us in the evil and the good that we do.' And like us, the Romans felt guilt rather than just shame, as in Seneca's play *Phaedra*: 'My guilty breast awaits the avenging sword'. Pilate was no doubt capable of this anguish, but I doubt he felt it about Jesus. How long might a Roman governor be troubled by the death of yet another Jewish messianic agitator? He rinsed those hands and they looked pristine enough for many — and perhaps for him.

Less successful at avoiding guilt was our Lady Macbeth, trying manically to scrub herself as she sleepwalked into the inferno. She wanted to take off the blood — not because her skin was marked, but because it was marked *to her.*

This was her own conscience, what Elizabethan theologian William Perkins called a 'little god sitting in the middle of mens hearts'. Interestingly, this idea was often taken from Romans like Seneca: our 'conscience' came from their 'conscientia'. This divine homunculus decided good and evil, moral purity and moral filth.

Here, guilt is wholly internal, not external. Yes, I am still smeared by the mud, slime, or crap of my own transgression. Yes, I still feel myself small, weak, and foolish next to what is great, strong, and wise. Yes, I still dread some punishment, either from god or society. ('Hell is murky!') But the wrathful spirit here is my own mind. I am the criminal and the judge.

In this, *Macbeth* is an oddly hopeful play. Despite its grim, nightmarish mood, it shows a noble lady mired by regret. Somehow, her 'little god' overcame her avarice and egotism. Losing her brutal numbness, she allowed herself to touch the stain of her contrition.

Which brings me back to my scholar, holding out *that* hand for me to clasp. In this, he is ritually and morally polluted. He has transgressed categorically, by combining what must not be combined. He has transgressed ethically, by putting others at risk of contagion. And with neither shame nor guilt to stop him, why would he not?

'Therein the patient / Must minister to himself.'

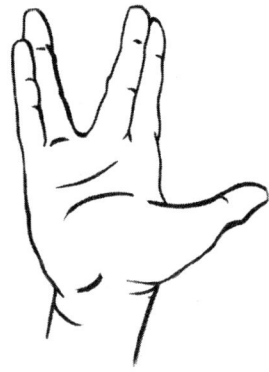

Fascinating

When my wife was ill (again) and needed urgent medical treatment (again), doctors put radioactive liquid into her. She entered a brutalist grey room with posters of that signature warning: three square-tipped triangles around a circle. The nurse kept away from her.

After leaving the clinic, she avoided our young children with their young cell nuclei; she avoided me, their carer. Before we drove home, she and I were divided by a thick window. She silently put her palm to the glass with her ring and middle fingers spread.

I understood immediately, though I did not cry (again).

Amok time

My wife was performing the so-called 'Vulcan salute', first seen in the premiere episode of *Star Trek*'s second season: 'Amok Time'. Throwing up his hand here is Lieutenant Commander Spock, who returns to his home planet for a sombre ritual. Suffering from 'pon farr' — a rut of sorts — he must mate, fight, or die of his urges.

The pon farr works dramatically because it is at odds with Spock's basic ethos. As a Vulcan, he is committed to logic. This is less the elimination of all emotions and more their Stoic subjection and sublimation. Vulcans are forever saying far less than they feel, and feeling so much more than they think they ought to. What Elena Ferrante wrote about Elinor Dashwood from *Sense and Sensibility* might be cautiously written of these aliens:

> She behaves like a lady who can confront a storm of individual feelings, with their egotistical impulses and ungovernable desperation, with an orderliness made up of ironic detachment and a spirit of observation. If, at a certain point, she allows room for sensibility and bursts into tears, it is only when she is sure that her own most secret anxieties will not disturb the life of anyone else.

Vulcans are a race of Elinors in a universe of Mariannes.

And in this universe, there is still adoration and loss. In 'Amok Time', our Elinor must fight his captain, James Kirk, in combat to the death. The ship's doctor makes it look like the Vulcan has killed Kirk. Believing he has taken the life of his best friend and commanding officer,

Spock is shaken. He salutes dutifully, then speaks to the officiating priest: 'Live long, T'Pau, and prosper.' She returns the courtesy, but Spock says he can neither live long nor prosper. Grieving and guilty, his life is likely to be shorter and lived with less dignity and pride. He might die of misery.

For all his rationality, Spock loves Kirk. Together with curmudgeonly Doctor McCoy, these officers are like a married threesome. When Spock greets his friend, there is genuine amity there — sometimes even joy.

This is why Spock gives his life for his captain and crew in a later film, and why this loss leaves Kirk stumbling, weeping. The Vulcan enters a radioactive chamber, knowing it will kill him and save the starship. Divided from his friend by a thick transparent pane, he holds his shaking palm to the window and spreads his fingers: the pinky and ring finger together, the index and middle finger together. A last Vulcan salute.

And this was my wife's message at the bus stop: *I am sick and sickening, and cannot touch you for fear of harming you — but I love you.*

Blessing

This fictional salute is not entirely fictional. It is older than Gene Roddenberry, who created *Star Trek*, older than his United States, older than his English language, older even than his Christianity.

The salute was invented by actor Leonard Nimoy. Or rather: Nimoy did the borrowing. Surrounded by artificial rock and actors in velour, he decided that the Vulcans were a manual people, a people of touching hands. So he used one half of a Jewish gesture he had seen as a boy: the spread hands of the kohanim, or priestly caste, as they blessed his family's Orthodox congregation.

This was the priestly blessing, or birkat kohanim in Hebrew. With their heads covered by prayer shawls, the kohanim held up their palms towards the gathering and spoke from the Torah: 'The Lord bless you and keep you; the Lord make his face shine on you and be gracious to you; the Lord turn his face toward you and give you peace.'

Spoken for well over two thousand years, these words offered a familiar hope for tranquil thriving. This was less about the eternal souls of Christianity and more about Israelites' safety and plenty in this life. While not uniquely Jewish, this benediction was certainly in keeping with the faith: looking to the Almighty for special succour and support. Not surprisingly this was also a way of warding off evil, those blessing hands spreading on amulets and talismans.

Observe the value of community here. For all the supposed magic in the air, the chief labour was social. For millennia, Jews continued *as* Jews. They were not monolithic or static, not one simple culture in one simple era. Judaism has typically been 'a heart of many rooms'. In the priestly blessing, believers came together to pursue flourishing, or to at least be reminded of the beauty in this pursuit.

But when 'Amok Time' was filmed, Jews were a significant but small part of the American population, with Orthodox communities being smaller still. Some had survived pogroms. Some had survived the Holocaust. All carried with them some of this ancient identity. They lived, still. But they were once again marginal, often liminal.

So for most viewers in the United States, the palm of the birkat kohanim was wholly new. It was not a familiar Catholic cross or raised goblet. And it was certainly not a Buddhist's mudra — Asians typically played servants or foreigners, not dramatic heroes. The sign of the Israelites was just exotic enough to be strange without being threatening; an 'other', but conveniently nearby.

Put another way, much of what Nimoy's dramatic gesture communicated originally was merely its alterity, its mark of oddness and remoteness. Ironically, the Jewish sign of common striving became outlandish: *this being is not one of us.*

Presence

Yet the ancient birkat kohanim was originally more than this simple sociological otherness. Its otherness was also ontological. It is said that the divine presence Himself shone above the priests' palms, that mortals encountered the Lord intimately. This is why the faithful were cautioned not to look at the kohanim, since the Almighty might damage them. (Like the posters in a clinic for radioactive treatment, warning of dangerous incandescence; like something beneficial that might kill you.)

Observe the shape of their hands: divided to let the light through. These were frames, which drew attention only to withdraw from attention — in favour of the blazing Almighty. The gestural language suggests a sublime fullness, an enormity that was beautiful but terrifying.

Here, the Lord was no ethereal spirit or abstract

ideal. He was a worldly force, felt beside and within the pious: shekhinah in Hebrew. In late antiquity, shekhinah became an independent personification of God; in modern Judaism, a feminist goddess. But in the older scriptures, the Almighty often arrived more primally as wind, storm, light. Fire was an especially divine virtue.

My point is not that the Lord had no body. For some Israelites, He had several bodies, even several selves — until the Torah's priestly authors decided otherwise.

My point is that the God felt during the birkat kohanim was as much overwhelming force as paternal persona. Even for the more conservative clerics, He was the original, originating face whose face blinded, the deity who turned to smoke those who offered smoke to Him. Yahweh was the ultimate beloved — who caused His lovers to squint, grimace, flinch: 'Thou canst not see my face: for there shall no man see me, and live.' He was not of our world, and was greeted by the wise with horror amid their joy. 'Apart from the terror,' Kierkegaard wrote, 'one does not know the great at all.'

This was what theologian Rudolf Otto called the 'mysterium tremendum et fascinans': alien, terrifying, seductive. Or as Spock might observe: fascinating.

Of course, the Lord no longer visits the temple as he once did — there is no temple to visit in Jerusalem, not even a tabernacle in the wilderness. Yet out of piety and respect, if not fear, Jews still must not look at the kohanim.

Leonard Nimoy looked.

He was drawn to the shekhinah, to an ecstatic eruption into the everyday, to something metaphysically more than a human, all-too-human community. In other words, he felt everything the Vulcan gesture was *not*.

(Do I believe he encountered the Almighty? No. No Almighty exists. Does this matter to understanding? No. You must read each 'no' emphatically, and with exhaustion.)

Conventions

The Vulcan salute is now more than the Hebrew blessing. In fact, it is more than the Vulcan salute. It now has a worldly significance, the hail of aficionados.

Since its beginnings, the *Star Trek* franchise has involved fan fervour. ('Fan': a seventeenth-century contraction of 'fanatic'. Someone mad, zealous, or demonically possessed.) When rumours of cancellation threatened a third season, a fan campaign began to defend the series: at least a hundred thousand letters and telegrams were received. Some simply praised the show. Some mocked the executives. Others wrote as extraterrestrials and threatened to destroy the planet.

The series' third season led to syndication, which in turn led to a life beyond the network. More shows and films followed, along with those refuges for common zeal: conventions. 'At my first convention,' wrote Nimoy, 'I walked into a hall so crowded, there was some concern the fire department would close it down.'

It is here that the Vulcan salute is most poignant. It is a way to greet or farewell that also acknowledges a common caprice: fandom. It does not simply address someone, but addresses them like-mindedly, recognises them as part of a social whole.

In this, it is what the Confucians called 'li'. This is best translated as 'ritual propriety', but also 'pattern' or 'path'. Li is the explicit sign that best suits the implicit circumstances, the text for this context. As in Aristotelian virtue ethics, this is not a matter of rules. Rather, it involves judgement, deciding the right time and place for the right gesture. 'Exemplary persons ... are neither bent on nor against anything,' said Confucius, 'rather, they go with what is appropriate.'

Importantly, what is appropriate — 'yi' in Chinese — is not simply social. It also involves personal feelings. This is partly why Confucius also emphasised shu: 'putting oneself in the other's place'.

So, you see someone dressed up as Commander Tuvok, leaning awkwardly by the wall in a noisy crowd. With shu, you feel for them, for their solitude in the throng of lime-green tunics and black jumpsuits with muted burgundy panels. You put away your toy phaser. With li and yi, you find a fitting hail. You hold up the Spock fingers without a smile, but with a raised eyebrow. Here, the gesture says: *welcome to our community of enthusiasm, fellow geek.*

But enthusiasts for what?

Utopia

Whatever edifying ideas its creator Gene Roddenberry may have occasionally had, the *Star Trek* franchise is primarily about entertainment. The casts and crews have used every possible trick to achieve this. Alongside expensive spectacle, they have tried smudged-lens beauty, brazen nudity, senseless violence, needless suspense, sentimentality, jingoism — sometimes even excellent writing. (One screenwriter to Roddenberry: 'Gene, you wouldn't know a good story if it was tattooed on the end of your prick.')

But insofar as the series and films are more than escapism, they offer a philosophical commitment. Spock's salute is shorthand for an ethical and political ideal.

This ideal is less about militarised, colonial Starfleet and more about the organisation it serves. The United Federation of Planets is a fictional union of sovereign democratic planets. Galactic liberal socialism. It offers the welfare and education of a collective, with guaranteed individual rights and liberties. A generation after Spock saluted T'Pau in his guilt and grief, Captain Picard summarised their politics with theatrical sonority: 'The acquisition of wealth is no longer the driving force in our lives. We work to better ourselves and the rest of humanity.'

The Federation's peace and universal suffrage did not arise from a few shining, thrumming widgets. This is a basic ontological mistake, believing that our technologies simply determine what we are. This is also a convenient error, since it allows elites to keep their power. They sell the promise of equality and justice with tomorrow's machines, leaving today's hierarchies of capital exactly as they are.

In reality, there is always a to and fro between us and our tools, each strengthening or stifling parts of the other. But only human beings can imagine ourselves otherwise — indeed, this is the very origin of democracy itself. Radical change in machinery requires an equally radical change in us. And *Star Trek* hints at this. The Federation's transporters are not emancipatory because they convert matter to energy, energy to matter. They are the common property of a liberated collective. Manu Saadia puts this neatly: 'What really matters, and what makes *Star Trek* uniquely utopian, is the social distribution of these impressive technologies.'

Within this utopia, citizens of the Federation are not ground down by poverty, sickness, and the ennui of empty labour. They are safe. This means they can proudly explore themselves and their worlds without today's risks.

Yes, this fictional premise is more radical than its writers and directors, who have most often viewed the future through white, male American eyes. Roddenberry wrote about equality while being a philandering bigot and chauvinist. But I am describing the charm of the stories, not the sordid realities they came from.

Here, another Vulcan ideal is often championed: infinite diversity in infinite combinations. While absurd if taken too literally, this maxim is best understood as a celebration of difference. We ought to welcome all the ways to be sapient; we ought to tolerate everything but intolerance. Put with Kirk's curt pragmatism: 'Here's one thing you can be sure of, mister: leave any bigotry in your quarters. There's no room for it on the bridge.'

So, in our world, the Vulcan hail is less the gesture of an alien race and more a pledge of humanism. It salutes our existence, and the recognition that this existence is *ours* to analyse and augment, denigrate and differentiate. Not atheism, but anti-theism. Most Federation citizens will not be told how to live, not even by omnipotent judges. We are the gods here — or we ought to be.

We raise our hands and part the fingers to salute our better selves.

Mongrel

What has become of this blessing? What has been lost or gained in the movement from Judaism to Hollywood to fandom?

It would be glib to describe the gesture's change as nothing but modern disenchantment. This too-neatly chisels the world into two brittle monoliths: religion with its shining sanctity, and humanism with its drab matters of fact.

Even the most cursory reading of the Torah reveals the value of ordinary customs. Yes, there is the flaming Father of Fathers, smoking in His tent. But there are also rules about building parapets on new houses, finding lost sheep, wearing wool and linen together, taking birds' eggs, eating a neighbour's grapes. 'When thou beatest thine olive tree, thou shalt not go over the boughs again: it shall be for the stranger, for the fatherless, and for the widow.' Even for the prophets, a holy life is not all holy.

Or rather, to continue over the generations, holiness must be made humdrum. The Israelites worked to exist through Hebrew and Yiddish, through the Torah and Mishnah, through circumcision and sitting shiva, through matzoh and gefilte fish, and so on — the whole miscellany of social life. The priestly blessing was both the ideal of this enterprise, and one common rite that kept it from extinction. Existence is a mongrel, sired by many modes.

Likewise, the typically rationalistic universe of *Star Trek* is also filled with divinity and piety. From its first series, the franchise has depicted godlike beings and worshippers. Yes, this was often condescending, seeing faith as an early waypoint on the journey to European science. But the tales and lore grew well beyond

Roddenberry's atheistic vision. They became more generous with religion, describing its devotions and rites with sympathy. Witness former guerrilla Major Kira Nerys: 'That's the thing about faith. If you don't have it, you can't understand it, and if you do — no explanation is necessary.' These stories are more sociological than theological, more about subjective beliefs than objective realities. Yet they still recognise the worth of spirituality alongside moral and political striving.

More importantly, *Star Trek* can also evoke the sacred. In the first film, Starfleet encounters an advanced alien craft, a living machine of unprecedented, unfathomable intelligence. Much of the movie features this being's overwhelming size and power. Spock is wonderstruck by this lifeform's logical precision, describing 'thought patterns of exactly perfect order'. He later weeps for it, fraternally.

The movie does not simply depict or discuss the sublime, as if this were merely more information. Instead, all of the cinematic crafts work to encourage awe in the audience. Expansive, exquisite shots of the *Enterprise* and the extraterrestrial ship have a devotional beauty to them, a mood of heightened cosmic astonishment.

Is *Star Trek* mostly created and appreciated in this mood? No. Adventure, kitsch, and moralism leave little room for transcendence. But enchantment is there, especially in moments of wide-eyed, wide-mouthed stillness. Space is dead — but not deadening.

And when fans salute one another, this is the cosmos that surrounds them: one of dutiful regimen and occasional gasping splendour. That is to say, a surprisingly religious cosmos.

Here, now

It would also be wrong to dismiss the Vulcan salute for its newness.

Yes, *Star Trek* is to the Abrahamic religions what a mortal is to the Lord: 'his days are as a shadow that passeth away'. And it is true that this fictional universe is more airy future than earthy past. Celebrating a grand socialist 'perhaps', its eschatology is mutualistic not messianic.

But it is a mistake to diminish the brief and recent, seeing profundity only in the lasting and old. Much that is poignant happens immediately and suddenly. Cosmically speaking, much that rightly gladdens or terrifies is very new. Isaac was new when his father had his hour of faith on Mount Moriah, when he put his knife to his only son. This does not lessen the horror of God's command or Abraham's obedience to it; it does not lessen the relief when the Almighty said, 'Lay not thine hand upon the lad.' Geological and ecological ages help to make sense of the planet, but they are no more real or worthwhile than the world of a blink. Nietzsche puts this with typical elegance: 'Against the value of that which never changes ... the value of the most ephemeral, the seductive flash of gold on the belly of the serpent *vita*.'

For gestures in general and Spock's in particular, significance does not scale with size.

Translation

Instead of shallow idealism or mayfly triviality, I understand Spock's raised, divided hand as a rough translation. That is to say, as a translation.

There is no perfect transformation of one language into another. This is not because these carry arcana known only to their adepts, but because they have different, disparate histories, because their grammar and semantics are not the same, because they have varied habits of suggestion and allusion. No master text sits above these, allowing for fast, final certainties. Borges: 'The concept of the "definitive text" corresponds only to religion or exhaustion.' And even in religion this is a contestable claim. Alas, the only way to correct someone's deciphering is with more deciphering. Versions upon versions upon versions, leaving some giddy.

This happens within cultures as much as between them; this happens within ourselves, because we are mixed in significance if not substance. How often do I write 'put another way' or 'put simply', translating myself? As George Steiner wrote, we are 'as crowded with contrasting impulse as Leonardo's drawings of the braids and spirals of live water'.

And yet. Translators float and dive in these currents, just as they have for millennia. There have always been those who live through more than one idiom, those who bring speech to hearer, page to reader, gesture to viewer — and vice versa. Where philosophy sees a problem, translators quite rightly see problem-solving.

Jewish American Leonard Nimoy was one of these polyglots. It was not enough to have a script for 'Amok Time'. The pages had to be turned into scenery, clothing, lighting; into the rhythm of speech and movement; into a quickly comprehensible but queer performance. To achieve this, Nimoy spoke in American English but gestured in Hebrew. In doing so, he translated extraterrestrial into earthly signs.

Yes, Vulcan is a fictional planet, peopled with fictional beings. Its rationalists in heavy make-up are made up. But imagined worlds are real in their way. Being imaginary is a manner of existing, not a kind of non-existence. Spock is not a real alien, but he is a real character in a real story: sitting at his black and pale blue fibreglass chair, peering into his scope.

And we can translate to and from this fictional world as we do others that involve the divine. Yahweh in heaven on his lapis-lazuli throne; Zeus in calm, clear-sky Olympus; one-eyed Odin on Hliðskjálf, watching all; red, bearded Brahma on his padma, his lotus; Inanna on her tree-seat carved by Gilgamesh; seated Isis, suckling Horus; Lord Itzamná in the netherworld, greeting mortal twins; all-powerful Ọlọrun, aloof in their transcendent sky. We cannot always celebrate the literal truths of these visions, but we lose little by this. There is still their perspicacity, beauty, poignancy; their power to enlighten, rouse, stir. Translations require only signs and their senses, not established facts.

Nimoy chose a largely unknown gesture for the largely unknown aliens. In this, he did what all translators do: he made something new. This was no longer the writer's script, and no longer the priestly hail. Soon, it was no longer even televisual, becoming widely sociable.

Does the raised hand translate between these perfectly? No, the stories and their situations are different; their ontological, political, and ethical emphases are different. Yet abstractly, the salute is surprisingly fitting. It is a formal blessing within a community, in which moments of awe punctuate getting-by. Spock's greeting neither distorts nor disparages the ancient Israelite original. And most in Nimoy's favour, his choice arose from wonder, not exoticism or nostalgia.

The Vulcan salute now exists somewhere between these three worlds: Judaism, fiction, fandom. It allows these to approach one another without touching completely — as if divided by glass.

Horns

Silk. Sequins. Stilettos. And someone else's hair.

For the shouting paparazzi, the singer glares, winks, pouts. Her name is called again, again, again. She grins, stick out her tongue — then raises her hand. But how? She makes no fist. She does not wave. And there is no salute. Instead, she holds down her middle and ring fingers with her thumb, and points to the photographers with her index and pinky.

Her gesture is neither warning nor a formal greeting. Instead, it is an avowal: *rock on*. Or, to make the implicit clumsily explicit: *do not hesitate before propriety or conservative mockery, just revel in the music and its lifestyle.*

This is the mano cornuta, or finger horns. And it has come a long way to the red carpet.

Evil eye

The finger horns arose in the heavy-metal scene, long before its mainstream success — before the bands had their own jets, bridges, documentaries. It still means more than casual celebration there, suggesting identity, affiliation, greeting or farewell, approval. One can throw up the horns to acknowledge oneself or the community, to claim music or tribe. One can use it like a wave: welcoming a fellow head-banger or doom-bringer. And one can use it like a grand, Nietzschean 'yes' to someone's guitar solo, drum riff, vocal scream.

The gesture is often associated with Satanism, with the fingers being Lucifer's horns. Certainly, the first performers to use it in concerts and album artwork were occultists. And legendary metal rockers Black Sabbath, who popularised the sign, were known to dabble in devilish iconography. Yet while other musicians were keen on demonic magicians, Black Sabbath were as much Catholic as Satanic. Yes, they sung of death, grief, decay, foreboding — but they also urged their listeners to save their souls, and to think of God as love. The mood was less like an actual black sabbath and more like Gothic literature: pagan rites taking place within a Christian universe.

The singer who made the finger horns famous was Ronnie James Dio. Needing his own schtick after Ozzy Osbourne left Black Sabbath, Dio forsook the peace signs for a gesture his Italian grandmother had used to 'ward off the evil eye'.

As a folk belief, the evil eye refers to curses and magical ill will. It kills newborns or beautiful brides; it seeks out anyone prominent for punishment. More primally, it is the basic danger of others, the basic fact of being vulnerable to their gaze. As subjects, these others — envious, malicious, cruel — have their own worlds, within which we are just objects.

How can we guard ourselves against this? We cannot. It is part of our psychological and sociological existence. But how can we *feel* like we are guarding ourselves against this? Feeling frozen by the other's look, we must move against them. We do this with rituals, charms, and gestures: exactly like the mano cornuta.

This is an old gesture, found across the Mediterranean. The mano cornuta has a handful of meanings, from the phallus to the threat of blinding. But its chief significance is as a defence against evil.

In Tarquinia, ancient Etruscan wall art shows two young dancers, naked or nearly so. He has a wine jug; she makes the high finger horns as she capers. Joie de vivre against decay and death. Two thousand years later, this occurs again in Filippo Lippi's fifteenth-century portrait of a noble couple, the fiancé making this sign at his wife-to-be's window. Another four centuries roll on and we witness the peasants in Bram Stoker's *Dracula*, knowing that a young Englishman is to meet the evil count.

> When we started, the crowd round the inn door ... all made the sign of the cross and pointed two fingers towards me. With some difficulty I got a fellow-passenger to tell me what they meant; he would not answer at first, but on learning that I was English, he explained that it was a charm or guard against the evil eye.

This is why Satanism is a muddled guide to the horns. This gesture is precisely what the devil is supposedly not: protective of the good.

Apotropaios

Like wide eyes, bared teeth, and tongues, horns are apotropaic: from the Greek for turning away, averting, banishing.

Apollo Apotropaios was a god of warding against evil. Standing at the city gates, the sun divinity stared at noxious spirits who might try to enter. Across cultures, apotropaic customs all have this primal significance. They arise from conflict, and how best to avoid it — or prevail in it. So we snarl, we scream, we point; we do all we can to make our foes flee, even if they are ethereal. Think of the bright blue eye found across the Mediterranean and Levant, hung from doors or necklaces, painted on aeroplanes. Each is a combative glare.

The horn is a metaphor for this aggression, and a metonym for our fantasies of it. We wear frightening masks and crowns. We hide behind these fiercer faces, then we simplify them. Just as the whole look becomes just a single eye, so too does the beast — bull, ram, stag, demon — become just a horn. It guards babies, newlyweds, even food. Then the horn becomes fingers, which stand in for it.

If we move back beyond classical civilisations, we find this sign again in ancient Egyptian art. The gesture's meaning is ambiguous, but shows a fallen Libyan soldier seeking escape from the wrath of the pharaoh. His finger horns might have referred to the god Baal and his equivalents across the Levant — as signs of sacrifice, victory or defeat, pleas for mercy. Whatever the specific significance, the general symbolism is clear: we do not grow horns, but we wear and gesture them to seek potency.

As apotropaic signs, horns offer power: in oneself and against others.

Metal

Music can be a practice of this very power.

It can encourage reveries of joyful potency, which Nietzsche called 'Dionysian'. In the thrumming beats and melodies, we feel a loss of self that is exhilarating rather than terrifying. Or perhaps a little frightening — but this is animating rather than paralysing. We merge with the song, one another, and seemingly with the cosmos itself. 'Singing and dancing,' Nietzsche wrote, 'man expresses himself as a member of a higher community: he has forgotten how to walk and talk, and is about to fly dancing into the heavens.' And who were Dionysos' companions? Satyrs: goat-men with prominent penises and prominent horns.

For all its iconography of doom, this is often the spirit of heavy metal. It offers vigour through music. It began in poor, working-class Britain, and was the song of furious, often melancholy young men. Having grown up with loud, filthy factories in bombed-out cities, they had little patience for hippy cheer. No sunshine of patchouli and major chords. Performing an orthodox masculinity, they were dark literally and figuratively: angry, fierce. And they set themselves against mainstream society. While heavy metal is now as much middle-class as proletarian, the music is still transgressive. It combines Dionysian excess with a message of blunt refusal.

The point is not that this scene is some gung-ho conspiracy, that metalheads are berserker criminals. They are no more aggressive than classical-music aficionados. And they often have high levels of connoisseurship, welcoming the music for its own sake.

The point is that metal is extreme in content and form, style and imagery. It does not want to console or beautify. It often wants to attack, and to revel in this. It is defined by its defiance. Ozzy Osbourne: 'To us, [flower power] was bullshit, living in the dreary, dismal, polluted town of Birmingham. We were very angry about it. We thought, *let's scare people*.'

So, the mano cornuta is more than a generic celebration of rock, more than merely *rock on*. It is also an apotropaic gesture. It provides a communal ward against helplessness and sadness. It offers a brazen metal message to parents, pastors, politicians: *fuck you, authorities*.

Cuckold

Yet the finger horns are also: *you got fucked*.

At least since the Renaissance, mano cornuta has been the sign of the cuckold. While England seems to have been especially fixated on horns, across Europe the two fingers behind a husband's head meant his wife had been elsewhere.

Consider the engraving *Cuckolded Husband Rocks Cradle While Wife Smokes*, printed in London in the first half of the seventeenth century. The couple are by the river, perhaps the Thames. The husband sits on a block of wood. The wife stands behind a table stacked with pipes. While our lady is busy with her tobacco, her aged spouse spins yarn and dotes on the baby. (*The* baby. Not *his* baby.) That is to say, the woman does supposedly masculine things, the man supposedly feminine things — the world is topsy-turvy. And as she stands there puffing away, her lover with his palms to her breasts, she is pointing at her husband with her right hand: little and index fingers straight at him. His back is turned, of course — his horns are secret to him.

It makes sense that the cheated-upon cannot see his horns and others can, that he is a figure of fun in his blithe innocence. But why horns? If these suggest potency and virility, surely the cheated-upon must lose his spikes?

Importantly, the cuckold does not simply have horns — he gains them. Or rather, he is given them by his wife and her lover. See Shakespeare's Benedick in *Much Ado About Nothing*, who scorns marriage. When Claudio suggests this bull Benedick might be yoked, the bachelor replies: 'The savage bull may; but if ever the sensible Benedick bear it, pluck off the bull's horns and set them in my forehead.' Matrimony turns studs into laughing-stock.

One theory is that these horns point back to Actaeon, from Greek myth. The lad spied the goddess Diana bathing and was turned into a deer as punishment. Wearing antlers, he was ripped to bits by his own hounds. This touches on the mano cornuta, but it fits the custom clumsily. Actaeon knew himself but was mistaken by others, while the cuckold was mistaken about himself and known by others. And Actaeon was tragic not comic

— a story to lament, not laugh about.

A better theory is that horns were thought to grow from semen in the brain. The more cum, the more cornutas. By filling the cuckold's wife with manly milk, the lover suckled the husband. (The white fluids were often conflated.) In other words, the woman was merely a pipe for the flow of sperm between men. Metaphorically, the three also became like polygamous beasts. Throughout the Mediterranean, billy-goats were a symbol of libido but also of licence. Hence the Spanish soldier Alatriste's mockery of a bailiff in *El Capitán Alatriste*, 'cornudo cabrón': cuckold bastard, but literally a horned goat. The betrayed husband is a laughable billy, not a noble ram.

Another theory is that cuckolds are like capons, fowl castrated for the table. The German for cuckold was 'Hahnrei', literally a rooster roebuck. In the sixteenth and seventeenth centuries, it was custom to cut off not only the bird's testes and combs, but also their spurs. These were then grafted to their head, making horns. While the etymological proof is weak, the symbolism is certainly strong: the cheated-upon gentleman is neutered like a cock with antlers.

Whatever the logic at work, the Renaissance cornuta are a sign of lost masculinity. These borrowed horns are no horns at all.

Dreams

But if we go further back beyond this era, we find more cornuta. From Artemidorus' *Oneirocritica*, written between the second and third centuries of the common era:

And someone said to a man who was engaged
and about to get married in a matter of days,
after he observed that he was sitting on a ram
and fell off it, that his wife would prostitute
herself and that, as the saying goes, she would
'make horns' for him.

Despite the centuries between then and now, this dream story is not vague. It has exactly the same iconography, with exactly the same significance: the cuckold has horns. It was written in the Mediterranean, where the gesture was certainly familiar. And the idea was already proverbial to the dream analyst and his audience. What did Artemidorus mean, thousands of years before the Renaissance began?

As always, caution is warranted. We are heirs to a mass of Greek and Roman culture, yet this legacy is a fraction of a fraction. We are handling tiny fragments of a world — and from within our own world. We can only speculate among the shards.

Artemidorus wrote that dreaming of horns arising from one's head was an augury of gruesome death. There is no talk of swapped semen here, no cosmology of milk and growths. So he did not believe that the lover gave the husband horns through the wife. And we have no evidence that the Greeks of late antiquity turned roosters into deer. Yes, they believed stags were angered by lust. After coupling, 'the deserted males rage in a fury of desire,' wrote Pliny. Yet this makes no distinction between success and failure, stud and cuckold. In short, the Renaissance cannot make sense of this classical gesture.

Perhaps it was carnivalesque? Having travelled

widely, Artemidorus may have witnessed the Roman Kalends of January, celebrated in Italy and later throughout the empire and abroad — even in medieval Muslim countries. What began as a local civic and domestic festival in Rome became something of a puckish fiesta in Christendom. It was not purely pagan, as Christians and perhaps Jews celebrated too. But it became wilder. During the masquerades, men sometimes wore women's clothes and antlers. They drank and screwed. Observe these familiar themes: reversals of traditional masculine and feminine roles, promiscuity, and horns. Maybe the Greeks saw cuckoldry as the fate of a reveller. While he wined and sang in his horns, his wife was partying in her own way.

Alas, Artemidorus was two centuries too early for these revelries. This was his culture's symbolism, but not his party.

At the risk of seeming too Freudian, perhaps it was all about penises. Like most Hellenes, Artemidorus knew the prick of good luck: a ward against evil. Greeks wore it, painted it, drew it as graffiti. The Romans also had the god Fascinus, who offered protection from fascination, from being seized by envy or malice. His totem was a phallus, often winged. Perhaps a husband worried by a wayward wife needed this sacred cock for luck. In other words, he gained a second knob alongside his own. And voila, the man had two horns, so to speak. If this is true, then the gesture made use of both mani cornute, apotropaic *and* cuckoldic.

I claim no conclusions here, only speculations. And one note: patriarchal paranoia is a stayer.

Lost horns

Another note: we are somewhat haunted by horns.

Behind the metal singer's raised fingers is an image that has cheered, enchanted, or goaded *Homo sapiens* for many centuries.

Throughout prehistory and history, these symbols — of might, fertility, arousal, protection, betrayal, and more — have pointed beyond themselves. Horns are pervasive. The ubiquity of bulls even casts doubt on the cult of stone-age goddesses. In Neolithic Anatolia, large aurochs with larger horns were chosen for ritual slaughter and decoration — perhaps a worship of masculine might. These kinds of bone spikes continued not only on altars and in friezes but also in our modern script. The 'alpha' in our 'alphabet' is from the Semitic 'aleph', or ox. And observe the horns on the Greek 'A': a Hellenic riff on a Semitic cover of an Egyptian original. Collectively and individually, we put horns on ourselves and one another.

We do not have horns, obviously. Yet we claim them — perhaps even covet them. Generation upon generation, millennium upon millenium, we signal with this aspect of animality. Megan Thee Stallion with hair horns. Sam Smith in a top hat with horns. Olivia Rodrigo collaged with giant hairclip horns. Post Malone with horns inked on his throat. Björk in coiled metal horns. And so on. From Neolithic temples to modern arenas, a continuity of bestial signs.

Yet there is no continuity of meaning, chiefly because Christianity made horns devilish. For many Europeans and those in their colonies, these spines hold mischief; they carry a sulfurous, diabolical whiff. Theist, agnostic, or atheist, the iconography still endures: of wickedness or at least naughtiness. Upon seeing them, even sober rationalists might feel what Arthur C. Clarke described as 'an ancient terror ... brush against their minds'. This is partly why the mano cornuta worked so well in metal music. If the musicians were not thoroughly Satanic, they were still projecting Lucifer's glow on their stage. The horns signified their transgression.

I have a mild longing to understand horns without this legacy. This might be encountering what the Minoans felt as their acrobats leapt over bulls. Think of Cretan author Nikos Kazantzakis at Knossos, the Bronze Age palace:

> Here the bullfight was a bloodless game. Man
> and bull played together. The bullfighter grasped
> the bull by the horns, the beast became angry
> and tossed his head high in the air, which
> enabled the bullfighter to gain momentum and
> jump with a nimble somersault onto the bull's
> back. Then he made a second somersault and
> landed on his feet behind the bull's tail, where a
> young girl was waiting to clasp him in her arms.

This might equally be the horns of Çatalhöyük, Memphis, the Indus Valley, Canaan, Gaul. And these were all bulls — saying nothing of rams, stags, goats, elephants. In China, the rhinoceros' keratin spike was exotically magical, and even used as a metaphor for Buddhism itself. Despite the symbolism, no sense of sin or vice arises here.

Even for we godless moderns, there is a vast pagan existence over which a thin sheen of trespass has condensed.

Cornucopia

Can I wipe off a little of this Christian patina?

Nietzsche once wrote of his astonishment at the Greek world, especially its 'moral free-mindedness'. As a people, they did not treat their souls as pure goodness, sullied by flesh. They recognised their uglier and more savage drives, and sublimated them into days, cults, games. Christianity came along when the Greeks had already lost this, offering these weary Europeans 'a balm'. Indeed, Nietzsche thought Socrates himself was proof of some spiritual illness, a malaise that left the Hellenes desperate for philosophy rather than their own graceful, easeful customs.

What interests me is less Nietzsche's analysis and more his awe: stepping back before another age and gasping at their otherness. He was especially sensitive to the past, not simply as scholarly history but as a testament to cultural brio. He also recognised that this was gone, partly because of Christianity, 'that disastrous lie of seduction'. He wrote of the grief of this, the loss of so much humanity, which can barely be known, let alone lived again.

This is how I feel about our ancient cosmos of horns. I feel amazement at what was, and melancholy that it is gone. Yet if I take anything from Nietzsche's cheery science, it not his bereavement but his joy: the feeling that we can suffer the fullness of history, and revel in this fullness. Eventually, we become strong enough to bear the whole past as ours. We wear this thick, pinching, rusting armour until it fits so well we can dance.

Eventually. Always eventually.

And for now? I raise the volume on Black Sabbath's 'Cornucopia' — and raise my little fleshy horns.

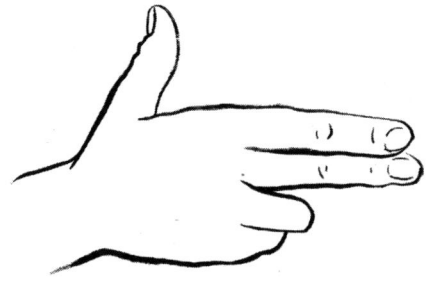

Pew Pew Pew

I am ten years old and having a treat. Lying on my belly on the fluffy flokati rug, I am watching the film *Blue Thunder* on the Blaupunkt. The German television has chunky modernist lines. The American gunship helicopter has chunky modernist lines. I am in a rapture.

I know nothing of the ethics of militarised police, of civilians treated like enemies. I just know that I love gunship helicopters with the aesthetic purity of a child who has never had to flee from them.

I also know the villain as soon as he enters: Colonel Cochrane. The Briton is blue-eyed and blond, his hair parted just so. Wearing a white turtleneck under a grey jumpsuit, he seems to sneer even when he is smiling. A full, smirking mouth.

Our hero is another laconic American officer, Frank Murphy. Murphy mocks Cochrane's educated accent. The Briton turns on his heel, points his finger like a pistol, then clicks a shot with his tongue: 'Catch you later.'

Later, Cochrane and Murphy argue in a car park. Sitting in his flashy Chevrolet Corvette, the Briton makes the same movement with the same phrase. Murphy looks surprised — perhaps even frightened. This man means him harm.

Towards the end of the film, the hero outflies the villain over Los Angeles. 'Catch you later,' Murphy says calmly, shooting with his finger and thumb — having just literally shot Cochrane out of the sky.

This was my cinematic introduction to the finger gun: a villain's farewell and a villain farewelled. It was not an accidental movement, not some idiosyncratic tic. Colonel Cochrane was precisely the kind of villain to use this gesture: a haughty arse.

Snap

This arrogance is universal, but its expressions vary.

Consider the finger snap. In Anglophone countries, it often means simplicity and rapidity. The middle finger and thumb literally move faster than a blink, conveying ease. In the *Avengers* films, Thanos vanishes people with a snap of his gauntleted hand — then Iron Man snaps them back. Just like that. While the conceited do click their fingers at waiters, the movement need not be rude at all. In fact, it can be celebratory. It has kept the beat for millennia in Europe, with ancient Greek musicians snapping their rhythms together. In *West Side Story* or *The Addams Family* or *Glee*, we join in without hesitation.

In Japan, the finger snap is much rarer in ordinary life. A foreign invention, it stands out for its sudden noise — an interruption and intrusion in a society known for its cultivation of silences. Yet the gesture is used with surprising gusto in the country's anime, chiefly because this features larger-than-life characters. The cocky young brawler Domon Kasshu in *Mobile Fighter G Gundam* snaps his fingers in episode after episode, also sneering and smirking. (And yelling: 'Shining Gundam!') This braggart with his bright red headband and cape is not simply showing how easily he beckons his mobile suit. He is also showing how easily he snubs polite customs. A brash outlander gesture for a Japanese milieu.

So, what is the milieu for Cochrane's finger guns?

Ouroboros

This seems like a military sign. Deployed in the macho banter between old soldiers, the pointing movement has a khaki tinge to it.

And the armed forces do have their own special signals. The United States Army developed a silent language for loud or clandestine operations. Some signs are iconic: raising the pinky and thumb to the mouth and ear, suggesting telephony. Others are emblematic: a thumbs up, showing a communication has been received. Others are indexical: pointing to the enemy with a rifle barrel or finger. What these have in common is the know-how of expertise. While simple pantomime works best with layfolk, the army are a specialised community with a specialised language. They share a lexicon.

But finger guns are far more widespread. In public life, we have politicians like Barack Obama and Joe Biden shooting liberally. In cinema and television: *Happy Gilmore*'s 'Shooter' McGavin and the eponymous Veronica Mars. The first is an arrogant, entitled boor who sprays his scorn all over the golf course. The second is a brave but vulnerable high-school detective who uses wit and snark as her shield. Very different personas, but the same gesture. Perhaps the finest fictional illustration comes from a Spider-Man film, in which a possessed Peter Parker dances smugly on the streets of New York. Like the jerk he (briefly) is, he pops his index fingers at strangers with glee.

These are not officers like Cochrane or Murphy. While they might command a nation's armed forces or punch bad guys, none are in the military — yet they all love a little phalangeal pew pew pew.

How easy to kill a man

Finger guns arise from where civilian paranoia meets military commerce, the American gun mythos.

Let me begin with a simple principle: firearms affirm antipathy. They are more likely to be used for intimidation than protection. They do not encourage calm; they prompt fear and aggression. They sharpen conflicts, rather than dulling them. While they might strengthen camaraderie between shooters, they only do so by firming up a new identity against others: the righteous gun owner. These relationships are chiefly about power. The shooter has it; those they shoot (or threaten to) do not.

This begins with a particular state of mind. Americans who buy guns are not doing so from some calm calculation of risk. Instead, they typically feel powerless, weak, and alone — seemingly helpless in the face of criminals around them. So they get guns for protection, mostly handguns.

Their fears are rarely realistic, however. They are threatened by an abstractly hostile world. White middle-class gun owners are worried that the authorities have abandoned them, and that killers or thieves are coming for them. In these visions of armed conflict, the attackers are typically people of colour. Put simply, this is a racist vision of black danger that justifies white violence. (In this fantasy, the villains do not look like Cochrane. Their eyes, hair, and skin are dark.)

Ironically, guns then worsen this state of mind by ramping up vigilance, vulnerability, and isolation. They make the anxious and lonely more so. But their symbolic worth is well known and obvious: they are talismans of strength and security. Firearms offer what design scholar Deyan Sudjic calls 'the flattering sense of being in command of an object that conveys authority and demands respect'. Their chunky modernist lines mean danger.

This is chiefly a fantasy for men. Most gun owners are men. Most gun killers are men. Most mass gun killers are men. Most victims of these killers are men. Most gun suicides are men. An ouroboros of coiled, well-oiled machismo.

Here, the firearm is a sign of power, but also of simplistic solutions to complex problems. A Real Man is strong and silent, with loose tactical pants and quick tactical draws. He avoids chatter. He avoids thought. He avoids showing feelings — except perhaps aggression. Best of all, he simply *does*: with perfect accuracy and somehow perfect morality. And for all the talk of protection, the longing for this vision of manhood is often far stronger than that for practical safety. Being a Real Man comes first. That is to say, being someone who can control others.

This is partly why some snipers speak of themselves as 'like gods': they can kill easily from afar. They need not strain and sweat to affect others. They can maim or kill literally with a curl of their finger. Likewise for school shooters, longing to be lords of life and death. Feeling like the world has wronged them somehow, they can revenge themselves with the ultimate power: deciding who may keep breathing.

Yes, many ordinary soldiers try to avoid harming their enemies. But firearms allow eager killers to do so simply, and without getting their hands dirty. This most personal of acts becomes 'strangely depersonalized', as psychologist and retired soldier Dave Grossman put it. Some even find this same moral simplicity while staring at the whites of someone's eyes. Witness Winston Churchill, writing from Sudan after pistolling a Dervish during a cavalry charge: 'How easy to kill a man!'

Historically, this is why gunpowder weapons were often mocked as unsightly and unfair. They killed very well indeed, and were proof of history's forward march. But they were for commoners who lacked the courage for tête-à-tête swordplay. That wise fool of chivalry Don Quixote lamented:

> in the heat of the courage and resolution that
> fires and animates the gallant breast, a stray

bullet appears, nobody knows how or from
where — fired perhaps by some fellow who took
fright at the flash of the fiendish contraption, and
fled — and in an instant put an end to the life
and loves of one who deserved to live for many a
long age.

While early handguns were clumsy, they nonetheless united death at a distance with convenience: tucked into a belt, under a coat. This is partly why they were seen as arms for poachers and blackguards during the Renaissance. They were for roamers and alley rats, those who hid while killing well beyond their reach.

My point is not that all trigger-pullers are chickenhawk losers — I was a sporting shooter myself. My point is that firearms in general, and pistols in particular, are as symbolic as they are practical. And what they so often symbolise is a fantasy of divine, sovereign will: deciding others' fates with merely a finger's twitch.

Vanity

Of course, finger guns cannot shoot. They aim at you, making a mere target of you — but they cannot shoot.

And this is exactly why the gesture means what it does. It borrows from the mythology and symbolism of firearm power — without even one grain of gunpowder.

In his discussion of pride, Aristotle distinguished between deficiency and excess on either side of the virtue. Someone without any love of self is pusillanimous, 'unduly humble'. A cringing thing, slinking away from noble deeds. Someone too fond of themselves is vain, from the Latin 'vānus': empty. Aristotle's Greek for vanity is a similar metaphor: chaunótēs, or porousness. The vain claim glories they have not won. Instead of being champions, they are all 'outward show', with nothing within.

Finger guns are a display of this emptiness. They are not vacant signs, but signs of vacancy. They suggest arrogance because they claim the very thing they lack: a chambered round, pointed at you.

This does not mean the gesture is always innocent. Torturer Mr Blonde in *Reservoir Dogs* uses it threateningly, as does our villain Cochrane. These finger guns are certainly a sign of malice. But this is malice as a pledge: a promise to do harm later, when the finger is on a real trigger. Observe the conceit here. Mr Blonde is not actually holding a pistol, but he will soon enough. And he is happy to wait — and to *tell* you he will wait.

The basic meaning of finger guns is this boldness, made bolder for its lack: *I have you in my sights (though I have no sights)*.

This meaning then shifts with character and context: hero to bad guy, sass to spite. Veronica Mars is cocky, and must be to succeed in her patriarchal town. Peter Parker with the Venom symbiote inside him is an egotist, lurching clumsily from milquetoast to jerk. Mr Blonde is a sadist, whose feigned trigger-pull suggests genuine violence. His smirking confidence is that of the psychopath, free from moral niceties. And our good friend Colonel Cochrane, the stereotypical Hollywood arsehole? A dollop of all three, with a pinch of posh accent for easily recognisable villainy.

What these characters all have in common is this: their hands assert command without actually being commanding. They are purest assertion. Perhaps, like Mr Blonde, they have a pistol under their coat. Perhaps, like Spider-Man, they loathe guns. What matters in the moment is that their hands are empty of steel — but not of significance.

In this, the finger guns are retaining part of their original milieu: the pointing, the pose of control. But they are not just repeating the whole bleak culture of intimidation and ragged individualism. There is a distance here between the world and its symbols, a distance that allows for some irony and play. That is to say, for a little hope.

Past tense

Long before the modern pistol was invented, archers shot at invaders through thin gaps in castle walls. Often called 'arrowslits', these holes allowed bowmen to harass, maim, and kill from afar. Sites of power with chunky premodern lines.

We often think of archery nostalgically now, with that soft dusk glow of history. The art has become a gentle sport, a weekend pursuit to exercise the back and arms outdoors. But in battle, bows and arrows were the original artillery: bringing terror from above. Writing of a fourteenth-century battle, English monk and chronicler Thomas Walsingham compared the fall of arrows to a dark cloud dimming the sun. Sixteenth-century English knight and military writer John Smythe wrote of arrows nailing men's feet to the earth.

As late as the nineteenth century, surgeons in the Americas were reporting dangerous wounds from indigenous archers. One doctor was puzzled by a

Mexican's cause of death, as there was no obvious mark on his skull. He found the cause upon autopsy: the man had been hit in the head, then had yanked out the shaft before he died. The arrowhead had stayed in his brain.

I add these details not to be ghoulish, but to be clear about the horror of these ancient weapons. Facing archers was often distressing and demoralising, causing the best to flee. Even mounted and armoured, those attacking fortified walls were pierced by the defenders' barbs — those commoners holding sticks and strings, hidden in their high little holes.

Another name for these slits: 'loopholes'.

As we use this word today, it is simply a surprising way of avoiding something, of being free from some necessity. The metaphor makes sense, as the ancient arrowslit and modern loophole are both small things with large consequences. We somehow make shocking escapes through each.

Yet in this old word, all the horror has gone — as if it vanished with the snap of fingers. It has nothing to do with bows and arrows, nothing to do with hard points puncturing bone and muscle, with cavalry horses, bucking mad from barbs in their flanks. A loophole is the husk of a trope, with all its living pulp scraped away.

This is what I want for finger guns: for the gesture to be understandable but utterly empty. I want its origins to be a historical curiosity, spoken about only in the past tense. A harmless legacy of that most American harm, the firearm.

Shush

In a suburban house in Colchester, baby Alfie is wailing in the kitchen.

His father, Craig, is not crying — not yet. But he cannot quieten the child. He feels a failure, this slob in his unironed, untucked shirt, buttons tight. His girlfriend does not think him able, and Craig frets that she is right. (She *is* right.)

But we need not fret. In the end of this *Doctor Who* episode, 'Closing Time', the father's affection saves them from death. Cyborgs try to turn Craig into one of them — he is clamped tightly into a conversion chamber, hard metal against his soft skin. Light flashes upon his face, purging his brain of emotions. But Craig's adoration for Alfie is too pure. He hears the child crying and — well, he loves his child. The alien devices explode, showing the power of feeling against anaesthetised machines. And so on.

All this is very ordinary, very now. I need nothing explained.

Another man is with the father and son, however: a collection of sharp angles with high, floppy hair. Serious overcoat, silly bow tie. It is the eponymous Doctor himself, and earlier in the kitchen he speaks baby. Turning to the child in his high chair, the Doctor puts his finger to his lips. Alfie is schtum immediately.

This I need explained. The trick only works on creatures with crude brains, the Doctor says. He later silences a department-store worker and Craig himself. All brains are crude to the Doctor, a time-travelling off-worlder with two hearts and many more selves. He is something of a mage.

Yet the sorcerous gesture he uses to shut humans up is not alien at all. Like ill-fitting business shirts with plastic buttons all the way down; like overworked bourgeois mothers and anxious, awkward fathers; like the belief in love overcoming the violent loss of self — this movement is so very familiar to me. *Of course* a nine-hundred-year-old extraterrestrial silences someone with his finger to his lips.

Time travel

Now, suppose I step into the Doctor's blue box and take a trip myself. First stop: Victorian England. They have little electricity, but bourgeois shirts still have mass-made buttons. Middle class mothers are not expected to work, but fathers are still aloof. And love? It is as capable of murder as redemption. I pick up a new tale by Henry James and read of a righteous young mother who lets her sickly son die rather than suffer his novelist father's corruptions. The narrator visits the family and approaches the mother — but the little boy is asleep. 'As I drew near she put her finger to her lips'. There is no ambiguity here: the mother bids him to be silent. Though I am a century from my own, I understand.

I leave crinoline and railways for Elizabethan Stratford-upon-Avon. Shirts are now pulled on, not done up. Sleeves are fastened with handmade buttons. The Renaissance family is cutting some feudal ties, so that many households are less clannish. These are not traditional modern families, but they are certainly smaller and more mobile than they once were. Old kinship strings are fraying among the poor too, so that many beg for public support instead of help from faraway relatives or aloof neighbours. Here, Craig might not find anyone to mind Alfie. In this age of transition, Shakespeare has anxious Prince Hamlet swear his friends to silence. To Horatio and Marcellus, the father-haunted royal says: 'Let us go in together, / And still your fingers on your lips, I pray.' Were I to shush the Globe theatre crowds in this way, they would know exactly what I meant. (And they would keep shouting anyway.)

Enough of this climate, tragic and damp. I flee to Assisi, in the High Middle Ages. In the Basilica of Saint Francis, I find men in grey habits labouring in their high-arched edifice. There are few buttons here, and fewer families. The Florentine artist Giotto paints an allegory in a vault of the Lower Church. Beneath the saint himself, Obedience sits in a loggia with her soft-edged square halo. Seated, in a blue cape, her salmon wings small, she rules between two-faced Prudence and quiet Humility. A monk kneels before her, and Obedience fastens a yoke on his neck with her right hand. At her lips is her index finger: silencing the sinners. I am now eight centuries from the schlub and his bub, but the iconography of quiet is still obvious.

And back I go, over the Mediterranean to Roman Numidia. And back I go, another twelve centuries. Finally, I have escaped Christendom for classical Africa. Someone is reading aloud the *Metamorphoses* of Apuleius. In this part of the tale, a Greek named Socrates has left his family and shacked up with an innkeeper, Meroe. His friend Aristomenes chastens him, telling him he deserves to suffer for this. Yet Socrates is terrified of Meroe, whom he believes to be a witch, and he begs his mate to say no more: 'he put his index finger to his lips, shocked and stunned: "Shhh! Quiet!" he said.' Almost two millennia between us, yet I still know this movement well.

Staying in Africa, I travel further into the past. I arrive before the Roman empire begins, in Ptolemaic Egypt. Wandering the catacombs for a little quiet, I find a small statuette of a child. He is naked, wearing a headcloth with a falcon atop it. This is probably the Greek god of silence, Harpokrates. Left hand in a fist by his side, his right is raised — to his lips, of course. In the same century, the Roman polymath Varro describes the deity for me: 'Harpocrates with his finger make a sign for me to be silent.'

Each of these eras asks for enormous knowledge — enough for a fictional chrononaut who stumbles from world to world, but too much for me. Only Craig and

Alfie's world is really mine. The rest dissolve into dark waters.

But the finger to the lips? It continues through these deep currents.

One simple digit

Can a finger actually stop us talking?

(And who are we? Not all species use sound to communicate. Bacteria and amoeba use chemical messaging, as do trees and fungi. Some fish use electricity. And within *Homo sapiens*, millions use signs instead of speech. They ask for silence without the finger to the lips. So my 'us' is selective: human beings who converse audibly.)

Of course, a finger cannot actually stop us talking.

More realistically, being physically silenced looks like the legendary monkey Iwazaru. A popular character in Japan, he famously keeps his hands over his mouth. Carved in the garish Tōshō-gū shrine in Nikkō, he is part of a trio: his friends do not see or hear, and he does not speak. He is not speaking no evil as the English saying suggests, so much as avoiding superfluous words. Perhaps he is also quietly criticising the authoritarian regime that commissioned his maker: mocking life under the Tokugawa shogunate. Whatever the rationale, no extra breath will escape these simian palms — Iwazaru is determined to mute himself. His lips are gripped tightly and doubly.

But gestures are rarely realistic in this way. Over time, they become simplified, and pantomime gives way to abstraction. To begin, I convey by pretending, performing. Perhaps I ape a monkey, clasping his own face; perhaps I drop to a crouch, stick out my lower jaw. Once we agree on this, my show can become more austere. It loses movement, detail. Eventually, I no longer need to mime at all — and now we have a sign.

And so it is with the Doctor's shush. It is a well-known and common token: *with this one simple digit, I suggest a well-covered mouth*. Through eras that were alien to one another, this sign has kept its simple familiarity.

Horus

But suppose I abide in Egypt, and travel back a few more centuries. In the sanctuary of the goddess Hathor, I find another statuette of a child: naked, wearing his boyish sidelock, his finger to his lips. He looks very similar to Harpokrates, this one. They might be twins. Whom is he silencing now?

Not a soul.

Because this is not a Greek or Roman deity; this is Horus. A popular god among Egyptians for thousands of years, this son of Osiris and Isis is identified with the pharaoh. He is a symbol of political legitimacy and powerful fertility. And his finger-to-the-lips gesture is not one of silence, but of youth.

Why did the Egyptians use this gesture for childhood? Was it a nod to finger-sucking, with which kids often soothe themselves? Is some subtle hieroglyphic pun being missed? I do not know, and neither do Egyptologists. But the gesture regularly marked young children in Egyptian art, rather than adults.

When the Hellenistic Greeks colonised Egypt, they

mistook this familiar gesture for their own: so Horus-the-child became Harpokrates, and the boy god became a divinity of quiet. Centuries later, the Romans still thought of this child as a symbol of swallowed sound. 'He keeps his finger on his lips,' wrote the Roman Greek Plutarch, 'in token of restrained speech or silence.' The Egyptian god was seemingly forgotten.

While the Greeks were certainly in power in the region, we cannot caricature them as aloof masters and the Egyptians as meek thralls. There was an enduring to-and-fro between these peoples. Many blurred neat colonial categories like Hellene and Egyptian, European sophisticate and African oik, rationality and savagery. Greeks also took up local gods: sometimes as they were, sometimes through a Greek double. Ptolemaic Egypt was a diverse nation, not an ethnocentric tyranny.

Yet the error is clear. The Greeks and then Romans never realised Horus was merely a child. That simple, so-obvious gesture made up their minds immediately — and did so for many lifetimes. Were the European literati simply too alienated from the provinces? Did they not care because it is the privilege of the conquerors to do what they will? 'How deliberately and recklessly,' wrote Nietzsche of the Romans, 'they brushed the dust off the wings of that butterfly that is called moment.' What happened to that fluttering Egyptian time? I do not know.

Egypt was often exoticised by the Hellenes, and it later became the alien 'other' for Europeans studying the Greeks. Despite generations of scholarship, this past is very much a foreign country to us. With questions of Horus and his raised finger, I must be comfortable with this answer for now: silence.

Without lifting a finger

It is a neat trick that the Doctor can gag simple-minded animals with a simpler gesture. An even neater trick: doing so without lifting a finger.

Europe could blithely take Horus as Harpokrates because Greece conquered Egypt and Rome conquered Greece. When the Latins were later vanquished by Germanic tribes, the child had been calling for quiet over at least seven centuries. Addressing shocked Christendom after Visigoths sacked the Eternal City, Augustine of Hippo wrote of the boy god in all the temples of Isis and Serapis: 'a finger pressed to its lips, apparently enjoining silence'. Why did the bishop believe Harpokrates was shushing worshippers? Because for him, these deities were just ordinary men who had been falsely deified. Augustine believed that pagans feared this truth being told, so they kept these shushing idols nearby to warn the faithful: *shut up about our counterfeit gods.*

Augustine was wrong about Horus and his Hellenic double, but right about silence: it often serves power.

This power need not be from phalanxes or swords. It is enough to believe in a common world, and to commit to this belief. The Greeks assumed a kinship between cities and citizenship, while the Romans did not. A Greek might die for Athens or Sparta; a Roman for the republic or empire. And beneath this? A basic conviction about common existence. This is what Pierre Bourdieu called 'illusio': treating seriously the game and its rules. We are raised, schooled, and trained to take for granted ways of thinking and feeling. We see these as not only ordinary, but also natural: part of the universe's fond, familiar workings.

Importantly, these workings need not be spoken about. In fact, we are often encouraged *not* to speak of them. Yes, sometimes this is achieved with simple violence. Retired to his estates after the rise of Caesar, Cicero lamented that armed louts had stopped him from orating freely. So he hoped to shelter and protect his 'orphan' eloquence in private. But there is also the coercion of etiquette, which decides the done thing to say. These customs sort the worldly from the naive, the urbane from the provincial, the polished from the crude. Witness Cicero the investor, putting his cash into agriculture. He understood these straightforwardly as commercial enterprises, rather than as pure rustic idylls. But he did not speak of these publicly, since it was coarse for his class to be too keen on coin.

Cicero was also known for his fine Latin, his sharp tongue often pinning the right words — before it was literally pinned by Fulvia. As Bourdieu noted, this is still so: speaking well and being heard are typically the privilege of the well-to-do. The beggarly are snubbed or laughed into quiet. More power. More silence.

But before threat, mockery, and contempt is convenient forgetfulness. More often than not, we ease into our lacunae. They are the stuff of ordinary, daily living: the cosmos of what need not be said. It was shruggingly obvious to the Greeks and Romans that thralls were part of life — 'to be civilized was to be a slave-owner,' as Alfred North Whitehead put it. How might a philosopher enjoy the good life if someone 'by nature a slave' did not serve him? There was typically no debate on this — not because the argument had been had, but because it had *not*. Despite that great Greek distinction between physis and nomos, nature and custom, some ideas were simply naturalised. This is perhaps why the Egyptians held so many beasts sacred, like Horus the falcon. These were symbols of ancient truths that were deeper than talk — that were too certain to be left to chatter.

So, the finger to the lips comes late, comes after those more profound silences. Like Iwazaru the monkey, we learn to shut ourselves up well before we are shushed.

Political animals

In the year Alexander invaded Egypt, his old teacher Aristotle died. Many of the philosopher's moral and political theories arose from the polis: the Greek city-state, so basic to their outlook. He was used to living and thinking within a smaller, more cheek-by-jowl community. Aristotle did not realise that the era of the polis was over, that sovereign city-states were giving way to empires exactly like his student's. The Greek who eventually wrote Alexander's biography would be a citizen of Rome.

Still, Aristotle was a keen observer of governance. And one of his most famous notes was this: 'man is by nature a political animal'. His point was not that we are merely selfish bastards, seeking gain for ourselves or our cliques; he was not a Hobbesian, inventing a primeval 'warre of every man against every man'. Aristotle argued that we are fundamentally social beings, and we cannot realise ourselves outside society. Put another way: he believed that we are not whole without one another. We are not full individuals who merely come together for protection — we more fully individuate together.

At best, we pursue this rationally. Our talent for speech allows us to 'set forth the expedient and the inexpedient', as Aristotle put it, 'and therefore likewise the just and the unjust'. If anything is 'natural' for us here, it is arguing about our common life.

Aristotle was not naive. He did not think that states are easily harmonious, that we are born into utopias of calm adoration. In fact, he argued that dissent and dispute were basic. We can stifle conversation with ridicule or cruelty, but we cannot do away with strife — and trying to do so often leads to more strife. For Aristotle, it was more 'natural' for citizens to have equal power and take turns in office. He was no modern democrat, and a tension exists in his work between suffrage and elitism. But he was closer to democracy than many believe, especially in his celebration of citizens' governance. Because politics is not a technical skill but a kind of prudence, all thinking beings can keep their hands on the polis' tiller.

Speech is not fair, of course. It is full of silences, like Aristotle's own prejudices about slaves — those beings trapped in the ship of state's hull. And language is not free, or free for everyone: many are estranged from their own tongue. But at the very least, Aristotle's ideas here are ambitious. If discord is always with us, then we ought to bring it into the commonwealth of talk. Or ought to try. We let our conflicts be heard and heeded, if not eased. This is how we share power.

An Aristotelian credo: be suspicious of those who refuse to listen.

Speechless

Which brings me back to the Doctor and his whiny familiar, Craig.

The Doctor does not need to listen, because he simply *knows*. He has ageless wisdom and arcane powers. Genetically superior. Intellectually superior. For all his monologues, he has no need of Aristotle's rational speech. He carries the Time Lord's burden from planet to planet, era to era. On a whim, he can shut us up with a finger to his lips.

What is unspoken and unthought behind this silence? The belief that we need an Übermensch to show us what is best in life, and that what is best in life is vulgarised Romanticism. The ancient prodigy in the bow tie — having skipped and stumbled from era to era, having witnessed horrific conflict, having himself fought in wars of extinction — shows us lesser beings that we simply need to feel the right feelings.

So Craig's love here is enough. He need do no more than simply emote.

The problem is not emotions, often trivialised in moral philosophy after Kant. It can be ethically praiseworthy to weep at tragedy and rage at evil. I am not celebrating Epictetus' Stoic custom: thinking of my child in the grave as I kiss them, so I will not be sad if they die. (A coward's trick. Not even Craig would stoop so low.)

The problem here is pure adoration celebrated as heroic resolution; is a father's affection alone as somehow revelatory and redeeming. Feeling is often the easy part, paternally — even Epictetus knew this. They are born, and we love them. The hard part is the daily grind of love: solicitude regardless of mood, and private care without public fanfare. This is love as changing nappies at dawn and feeding at midnight, then the seemingly endless cycles of laundry, cooking, cleaning — to say nothing of the conversations (or worse, the silences). Like many wonders, fatherhood is also a wearying, sometimes harrowing labour. Craig cannot even clean up after himself for a few days. The Doctor's shushing finger symbolises this condescending sentimentality.

I am indeed speechless — though not with gratitude.

Gills, Glass

It is ordinary for him to arrive at the corner house in the late afternoon, after his classes. Ordinary for him to walk past the *Ginkgo biloba* sapling growing slowly by the carport. Ordinary for him to peek into the garage studio, to see what the painter has done. And ordinary for him to walk idly past the bedroom windows that face the concrete path, thinking already of the stovetop coffee he will brew once inside.

Magpie ululations, traffic from the highway nearby, a circular saw: all taken for granted.

But her sweaty chest; her knees gripping hips; her dark hair lank with effort? This is not what he had expected. By the time he realises what he is seeing through the reflections — his friend and her boyfriend on her bed — it is too late. He moves to the kitchen quickly and seeks his ground beans.

Perhaps an hour later, she joins him at the table.

She allows her face to grow slack. Widens her eyes. Opens and closes her lips. And pivots her hands to and fro under her chin. In a relaxed rhythm, her mouth gapes and her palms turn together.

He has never seen this gesture before — it is charming but alien. Yet he recognises it immediately, because it is a simple pantomime. She is saying silently: *I now feel like a goldfish in a bowl*.

Panopticon

As she flutters her hands beside her throat, his friend is using the goldfish's world to make sense of her own. And this sense can be boiled down to three things: glass, water, and stark simplicity.

We use glass to keep the animal controlled and observed. It is similar to what nineteenth-century British philosopher Jeremy Bentham called a Panopticon, from the Greek for 'all-seeing'. Bentham meant it for men, not fish, of course — and he meant it happily. 'The more constantly the persons to be inspected are under the eyes of the persons who should inspect them,' wrote the father of Utilitarianism, 'the more perfectly will the purpose of the establishment have been attained.' Bowls and tanks have glass because bars will not do for scaled prisoners. But the principle is the same: contained visibility.

Also, observe her movements in the water: slow, rather than rapid; stilled rather than in motion. She is floating without firm concrete or carpet from which to flee him. And she feels weak, trying to push on through fluid instead of thin gas. The overall impression is of drifting, disoriented suspension: exactly what it is like for a human being stuck in a bowl full of liquid.

And think of the fishbowl's limpid austerity: without rain or sun, tides or currents, predators or prey. Just container, water, animal. This is how the American thinker William James caricatured absolute idealism in philosophy: 'an aquarium, a crystal globe in which goldfish are swimming'. This was another way of saying that this philosophy was too abstract, too lacking in the mess and flow of actual empirical life. All form and no substance. Likewise, having seen the voyeur at her window, his friend feels like most of her world has dropped away. She is reduced to awkward severity, merely a creature in its clear receptacle.

So, the fish is not here to speak for the fish. It is a trope for a very human state of mind: *I feel surveilled and captivated.*

The look

Being watched can certainly feel arresting, like we are somehow restricted, restrained.

Yes, if I am part of an elite, I might be witnessed as such, seen in all my glory from afar. Think of the Grand Hôtel that Marcel Proust describes, full of the wealthy and highborn: 'an immense and wonderful aquarium against whose wall of glass the working population of Balbec ... pressed their faces to watch'. But if I am powerless, the glass fixes rather than fortifies me. I live in fear of being *seen*.

And this anxiety is often enough alone, without the need for absolute surveillance. Ever the enlightened patriarch of the poor or colonised, Bentham took this for granted as a boon of his Panopticon: 'at every instant, seeing reason to believe as much, and not being able to satisfy himself to the contrary, he should conceive himself to be [watched].' This logic occurs not only in prisons, but also in schools, the military, medicine, corporations. I carry my guard's look inside myself — or my principal's, my officer's, my psychiatrist's, my boss's. In what French philosopher Michel Foucault called 'the punitive society', institutions encourage me to see myself through their eyes. My sense of self becomes something they define and measure, something that only exists because they qualify and quantify it. They need not coerce me if they can help to create me.

Yet this would fail if I were not already vulnerable to the gaze — to your gaze. Part of being *Homo sapiens* is being with others. Not every now and then, but always — even when we are alone, others are alongside us. And this togetherness is not easy. Each of us has our own little cosmos of being — and we *know* that we do. So when I am witnessed by you, I feel myself in your orbit. I become less of a subject and more of an object; a thing, drawn to your centre of gravity.

This would not happen if I were really just stuff. It is only because I am a (somewhat) free consciousness that I can think of myself otherwise. But when I see myself through your look, I become aware of myself as a lump of matter, not spirit. I become a chunk of anything but freedom. Discussing the shock of puberty, the philosopher and novelist Simone de Beauvoir put this eloquently in *The Second Sex*:

> The young girl feels that her body is getting away
> from her, it is no longer the straightforward
> expression of her individuality; it becomes
> foreign to her; and at the same time she becomes
> for others a thing: on the street men follow her
> with their eyes and comment on her anatomy.
> She would like to be invisible; it frightens her to
> become flesh and to show her flesh.

As this suggests, often others' gaze leads to shame. Think of his friend in her bedroom, blissful and celebratory — then she sees him looking through her window. Suddenly she sees herself as he sees her: merely a body among bodies. 'The body symbolises here our defenceless state as objects,' Jean-Paul Sartre writes. 'To put on clothes is to hide one's object-state; it is to claim the right of seeing without being seen.' Without her clothes, she is just however many kilograms of flesh: flushing, sweating, and oozing.

Now she is apprehended in both senses of the word — cognised by him, but also captivated.

And what of her gilled gesture? No blushing conservative, she enjoys her carnality. And she lacks Sartre's cringing dualism, his loathing of flesh in general and his own flesh in particular. Yet she is feeling something akin to this. While screwing, she is revelling in her corpus, becoming aware of herself as body, freely and with joy. She is not wholly flesh here. She is savouring an ambiguity between mind and body, subjectivity and objectivity, restless becoming and contented being.

His voyeur's eyes collapse this ambiguity, and she becomes purely a skeleton wrapped in moist muck. If not shame, she is now feeling its cousin: embarrassment or humiliation. The goldfish is a symbol of her visceral capture.

Feral

Where does this metaphor come from? Partially her mind, obviously. But partially from the world too. And one of the hallmarks of the world is its taken-for-grantedness, the way it is just so and always has been.

And as always, this is false.

She beds her boyfriend and makes fish faces on the Mornington Peninsula, over rocks that were formed roughly half a billion years ago. The Boon Wurrung or Bunurong people of the Kulin Nation settled the area at least forty millennia before she was born.

Next to these spans, goldfish only just arrived.

Well over a thousand years ago, they were originally bred in China from carp. Beginning as grey or black spawn, with maturity the fish gained their lustre: from dullness to gilt glory. Whether they were prized for their beauty or their seemingly magic transformation, they were not for hoi polloi. Chinese commoners in the Song Dynasty were banned from keeping the gleaming things, which were reserved for royal ponds. Later, all Chinese were allowed to keep them: in pools, pots, and bowls. By the eighteenth century, goldfish were a typical sight on woodblock prints, a symbol of prosperity and success in civil examinations.

Goldfish were introduced to Japan in the sixteenth century and Europe in the seventeenth. A similar déclassé descent followed: from elite to common patronage. Only Japanese nobles and samurai were allowed to keep koi until the Meiji period, centuries later. In England and the continent, they were imperial spoils for scientific gentlemen or connoisseurs. Their popularity as upper-middle-class pets rose in the nineteenth century, when fancy fish were marks of wealth, taste, and good breeding. This is partly why Proust was familiar with these aquarium curios: he was of a class that welcomed exotic Oriental goods like kimonos, cloisonné, pith miniatures, and bonsai.

But not all goldfish owners were well born. In the same period, the new United States Commission on Fisheries received a huge delivery of ordinary Japanese goldfish stock, and gave them away: some tens of thousands. And nothing rubs off the elite sparkle like the masses enjoying something too. By the twentieth century, the fish had lost their posh shine in Anglophone countries. So goldfish soon became symbols of either lost Gilded Age decadence or new lower-class domesticity. In the first year of the United States' Great Depression, tens of millions were bred every year. This is the era of goldfish in plastic bags carried home from fairs, of carp as suburban pets in factory-manufactured glass bowls.

In Australia, the fish were introduced from Japan in the second half of the nineteenth century. The former lands had been invaded by British sailing ships; the latter by American steamships. Imperialism met colonialism, and one result was goldfish ornamenting Antipodean ponds. They are now feral in the country, taking over not only freshwater rivers and lakes, but also brackish estuary waters.

So, his friend's gesture only makes sense as part of a larger story of forced change: humans remaking species and territories. The little carp had to be bred then shipped between empires before it became a common-sense suburban trope.

Goldfish

And what does it feel like to be this goldfish?

Phrased this way, the question is like philosopher Thomas Nagel's: 'What does it feel like to be a bat?' Nagel's answer is that we know little about its subjective life, despite all we can describe about it objectively. Yes, the little fish has sensitive colour vision, and can see ultraviolet colours we cannot. Yes, it uses its gas bladder to hear at low frequencies. And, yes, it can make memories very well indeed: spatial snapshots of situations, just like us. But what are these sights, sounds, and maps like *for* the fish?

Put simply, a third-person fact about an animal is still a fact — but it is not a first-person fact. Through experimental research, we can get a very thorough idea of the fish, but we cannot get an equally thorough idea of the fish's ideas. 'These experiences ... have in each case a subjective character,' Nagel writes, 'which is beyond our ability to conceive.'

Philosophically, Nagel is not that interested in bats, let alone fish. It is *Homo sapiens* that most concerns him. His point is not that cave flappers and tank swimmers are enigmas to us, but that we are enigmas to ourselves. He is taking to task popular beliefs in neuroscience: that objective studies of brains tell us everything about our subjectivity. Scans of neural tissue and blood flows are not illustrations of our consciousness. They tell us a great deal about our physical make-up — they tell us very little about *what it is like* to have this physical make-up.

Yet Nagel's arguments also change our understanding of other animals. Or rather, they show how difficult it is to understand how other animals understand. This is why the German biologist Jakob von Uexküll maintained that there are as many worlds as there are species. Every kind of animal senses, perceives, and responds to the world differently — and so there is no one simple cosmos out there, within which all life roams.

To make sense of this, Uexküll popularised the concept of the Umwelt, which can be translated as 'environment' or 'environment-world'. This is not like a large empty box within which organisms rattle around together. Partly created by different organs, physiological needs, and life courses, the Umwelt is 'a piece cut out of its surroundings'.

Even time changes from one Umwelt to another. Uexküll observes that some fish do not recognise themselves if they are shown their likeness less than thirty times a second. Their moments are quicker than ours — and they must be for them to catch their swift prey. Slower animals do not matter in the same way, if at all. The same is true for human beings. We often do not notice the slow industry and intricacy of plants. They become merely compliant wallpaper or defiant furniture.

Because the warp of these Umwelt lenses are so familiar, they can even skew what experts see. These radical differences are overlooked in scholarship: they miss distinctive sensations, values, categories. Like all species, we are so very worlded.

The Umwelt is not a reason to give up on realism. It is through careful scientific research that we can establish the worlds of fish and bats. In other words, it is objective study that suggests our very subjectivity. And perhaps some species can become a little more intimate by working together. Falcons and falconers learn about one another's minds, as do dogs and their humans. Still, we ought to recognise that our run-of-the-mill reality is *ours* — it is foreign to other primates, let alone to finned bowl-circlers.

Yes, the fish's placid otherness can be a boon of sorts, as philosopher Patrick Stokes observes. Staring at goldfish, with their wide-eyed oddness, can help us withdraw from our own fixations and manias. But a genuine otherness it is.

In short, we do not know how goldfish feel.

A piece cut out of their surroundings

So, the goldfish is an impromptu sign of his friend's self dropping away, of the sense that her consciousness is trapped and drowning. But the symbol itself relies on the goldfish's self dropping away, on our fantasies of capture and filled lungs, encouraged by the colonial spread. The animal's gilled buoyancy has gone.

She and he understand the gesture immediately, because they are the same species with a culture in common. The goldfish is part of neither: it is stuck within their Umwelt, but not of it.

Like the Umwelt, metaphors too are a piece cut out of their surroundings.

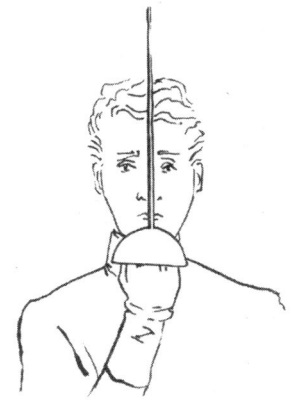

Savage Noble

Come closer, friend. Because you want to hit me — and I you.

We each hold a broadsword, roughly a kilogram of metal, wood, and tanned hide. This is relatively light — weighing less than my newborns once did — but it has heft when swung. Allow me to anthropomorphise: it is single-minded, sniff-necked, pig-headed. It wants to continue in such-and-such a direction, and often this direction will be *through* one of us. Physics hurts.

And so.

Here we are, the two of us: perhaps a few paces apart in the park, in the shade of an old oak. We cannot yet reach one another, but we soon will. Perhaps you hope to smash your broadsword down onto my forehead. If so, I hope to slash up into your fingers or wrist.

My pulse has quickened already. I am ready to hit you. Indeed, I *want* to hit you.

But before the violence begins, I pause. Sword pointing up, I raise my hilt to my face with the knuckles towards me. Then I sweep the sword down and across my body so that it points to the yellowing grass.

But why?

Swords are cool

Yes, I do enjoy waving blades about.

And this is no idiosyncratic kink. Swords have been feted for many centuries, at least in Western Europe. In the hands of royals: the garish British Sword of State that made a prince of the Prince of Wales; or Joyeuse in the Louvre, the golden sword supposedly swung by Charlemagne himself ('girt about him ... his peerless blade, / That changes colour full thirty times a day'). In literature: Beowulf's Hrunting ('annealed in venom and tempered in blood') or King Arthur's Excalibur ('brightly burnished'). In cinema: Conan the barbarian's atavistic bastard sword with its snarling fish hilt, or the pulsing, humming Jedi lightsaber that suggests a lost elite.

In short, swords are cool.

This is partly because they are aesthetically pleasing: keen curves or straight lines, shining metal, elaborate or austere hilts. Also the felt beauty of balance; the way the broadsword leans into the cut, or the rapier into the thrust. When you pick it up, you *know* — only this knowledge is felt, not thought. Consider Richard Sharpe's covetous esteem during the Napoleonic wars:

> God, but he wanted it! He had handled the
> weapon during the night, feeling its balance,
> knowing the power of the plain, shining steel,
> and Sharpe had felt the lust to own this sword.
> This was a thing of lethal beauty, made by a
> master, worthy of a great fighter.

There is certainly this thrill in the raise and sweep of my broadsword, in the way the heavy hilt and lighter blade give themselves to the swift whipping arc.

Historically, swords have also suggested virtues, like perseverance and courage. While arrows and bullets kill from afar, the sword-wielder must put themselves in obvious danger. As Victorian adventurer and translator Richard Burton put it, 'the shorter the weapon the braver the wielder'. Daggers are equally intimate of course, but sneaky. They speak of guile, not valour.

Swords are wearable too, which makes them part of our social identities. In this way, martial (and masculine) symbolism becomes stylistic. What begins as a sharp stick ends as couture. Diarist Samuel Pepys, cutting a fine Easter Sunday figure in seventeenth-century London: 'Up and this day put on my close-kneed coloured suit, which, with new stockings of the colour, with belt, and new gilt-handled sword, is very handsome.' I might carry a halberd or longbow to war, but I swagger in the city with a sword at my hip.

So, swords are pleasing things that imply personal excellence, and make this implication chic. This sheds light on why you and I are swinging broadswords at one another, and on the mere fact of our enthusiasm.

But it leaves the gesture itself dim. Why am I raising and sweeping my blade at you? Why not just have at it?

Do you thumb your nose, sir?

Perhaps I hope to goad you into angry distraction, to leave you swinging furiously instead of parrying and riposting. Here, my movements are a slight, meant to start strife. Think of *Romeo and Juliet*'s cock-punning bravos, looking for trouble on Verona's streets. 'I will bite my thumb at them,' says Sampson, 'which is a disgrace to them, if they bear it.'

No, neither of us bite our thumbs — unless they are swollen. (They might well be soon.) This is just an ordinary salute. While originally a verbal greeting of good wishes or homage, 'salute' now typically refers to gestures alone. Yet the fourteenth-century ideas of fellow feeling, esteem, and courtesy remain. In other words, the salute is the exact antithesis of Sampson's Elizabethan obscenity. It is a gesture of recognition, not rudeness.

With our swords, we are showing each other polite regard.

Fencing

This is because we are fencing, you and I.

Our broadswords and drills come from Shakespeare's era like Sampson, but our salute comes from the eighteenth century. Then, fencers were often expected to perform something between a demonstration and dance. Fleet Street fencing professor Jean Olivier called it 'an usage established in all the fencing schools, in order to preserve the politeness that we owe another'. French-schooled, Italian-born master Domenico Angelo devoted several pages to the salute, which included hat-doffing, foot-tapping, and various parries and guards. It was a sign of respect to one's partner and the spectators, and Angelo was quite clear about its manner: 'a genteel deportment and a graceful air are absolutely necessary to execute this.' No doubt this was the perfect outlook for Eton's fencing master. Despite his foreign birth and residence, Angelo's treatise was also taken as exemplary by many French: the philosophers Denis Diderot and Jean le Rond D'Alembert used his work for their *Encyclopédie*.

Centuries later, modern sport-fencing competitors *must* salute one another before they bout — or risk exclusion from the match, and suspension from the tournament. Their gesture is simpler than Olivier's and Angelo's, but still marks the contest.

The meaning of the movement is chiefly in its intimacy, the way it relates combatants to one another. Common to all European fencing salutes are two simple but striking movements: I raise the sword, then sweep it aside and down. Here, the weapon begins either before my face or pointed towards yours — both positions protect me. But then my blade is swept away. Even when this movement is a parry, it leaves me suddenly facing you without steel between us. I am now open to harm, as are you. And yet we stay.

A similar logic works in a Filipino martial salute, seen in the film *Dune*. When Timothée Chalamet and Jason Momoa put their daggers to their hearts then foreheads, they are signalling their sincerity *and* susceptibility.

So, the blade is a mediator here. It points to the situation and those involved in it. It nods to our shared fencing reality: *here we are, you and I — vulnerable to one another but brave.* This is its courtesy, even as competitors try to thwack or poke one another.

Duelling

But fencing was not simply for sport. It arose from a nastier pursuit: duelling. Hence the need for defence, whence we have the word 'fence' in English.

Masters like Olivier and Angelo were not carrying broadswords but smallswords: lighter, thinner, shorter cousins of the rapier. While these were typically worn by officers in the eighteenth and nineteenth centuries, they were not battlefield swords. They were chiefly for killing privately, and most fencing is concerned with this, the one-on-one encounter.

Here, the duel is neither a fracas nor a skirmish. And the duellist cannot sneak up in an alley to put poisoned steel into an enemy's calves or spine. It is formalised, ritualised combat — typically between two gentlemen. One-on-one fights were known in the ancient eras, like Hector and Achilles or David and Goliath. But the modern duel is a very specific kind of bout, which arose in a very specific age: sixteenth-century Italy. In other words, it is a Renaissance invention.

In cities like Verona, aristocratic chivalry and pride met bourgeois individualism. The nobles' medieval power was being usurped by states on one side and merchants on the other. Responsibility and blame shifted to persons instead of whole families, and to royal law instead of divine right. Yet aristocrats still wanted to protect their honour as gentlemen and as clans — their right to revenge, without meddling kings or courts. Duelling gave them this, but made it codified and public. It helped to 'preserve the illusions of those too civilised to celebrate pure savagery', as one novelist put it. If they wanted to draw blood from someone who bit their thumb like Sampson, they had to do so formally and with witnesses. Brawling was for commoners, and a dagger in the kidneys for cowards — gentlefolk duelled.

The middle classes also crossed swords, though they were not protected by law. Think of Florentine goldsmith and memoirist Benvenuto Cellini, a violent braggart who handled steel just as well as the softer metals. After duelling in Florence and angering a mob, Cellini and his brother were exiled from the city for six months. Many citizens carried blades, but only aristocrats used them with royal favour and pardon.

The duello spread quickly across Europe, though especially in France. Here, duelling became a purely upper-class pastime. During the reign of Henri IV, perhaps more than four thousand blue bloods were exsanguinated by other blue bloods. The British Isles eventually turned away from 'going out', as they called it — the sober, more sensitive Christian gentleman offered another ideal. But from the seventeenth to early nineteenth centuries, they were as keen as their friends across the channel.

This became one of the hallmarks of the aristocracy, a distinction of the international elite. With this tête-à-tête, they shored up their specialness. Battles were now won with massed pikes, archers, and cannons — but these gentlemen risked rapiers at dawn. Nobles were born to unearned wealth and undeserved privilege — yet they were willing to die over a quip. Yes, commoners were torn to pieces by gunpowder and trampled by horses — but nobles drew their swords with polite calm.

It was absurd at times. In fiction: a marine and a ship's surgeon challenged one another because the former's dog ate a pickled hand belonging to the latter. In fact: two officers duelled after their Newfoundland dogs fought in

Hyde Park. After one of these men died from his wounds, the other was tried for murder and defended himself in this way: 'It is impossible to define in terms the proper feelings of a gentleman; but their existence has supported this country for many ages, and she might perish if they were lost.' He was found not guilty.

With this absurdity, the elite protected themselves. Firstly, as gentlefolk: vying against one another, they gained glory with bravery. Secondly, as a whole class. The higher one's status, the less one is supposed to care about ordinary utility, to pause for the calculations and negotiations that keep us alive. The middle classes would scorn 'the follies and the crimes, the plunder and the waste', but of course they would. It was bourgeois to count pennies, to avoid gambling, to keep only one bedmate. The nobility gracefully threw away coins and mistresses — and their lives. In doing so, they proved their devotion to their cohort.

In this way, duelling was a symbol against which law, Christian morality, and even common sense were powerless. Witness D'Artagnan the elder's counsel for his son:

> I have taught you to handle a sword; you have legs of iron, a wrist of steel; fight whenever you can; fight the more for duels being forbidden, and therefore it takes twice as much courage to fight.

Though D'Artagnan's father was the caricature of a rash Gascon, *The Three Musketeers* was written while Frenchmen were still shooting one another over trivia. This mindset seemingly denied kings as well as plebs, and gave the aristocracy an aura of fateful courage. Yes, it was useful for monarchs to celebrate upper-class virtues while taking middle-class gold. This was what sociologist Norbert Elias called a 'royal mechanism', in which competing cohorts were played off against one another for regal benefit. Yet for the nobles themselves, this was often more atavistic than practical. 'Any élite guilty of elevating itself above the level of common humanity is liable to inflict unnatural penalties on itself,' writes historian V.G. Kiernan. 'On the field of honour the dominant class sought, in effect to expiate its collective sins.' For the ruling echelons, the duel was a modern sacrifice, in which they tossed a few corpses to their god: society.

So, the duel's salute has a dual significance. It bears witness to your nerves of steel — you, who might soon be dying by my steel. It respects your stiff upper lip in this martial moment, though you might be a scrub or harlot in all others. At the very least, it allows me to seem more manly at the club. But it also hails our tiny commonwealth, blessed by Angelo's 'genteel deportment and a graceful air'. Put another way, we are saluting one another, and we are also *not* saluting others: the petit bourgeois worker, the petty officer, the Jew, the lady. In this world, they have not lost their honour — they never had it to begin with.

Yet you and I are commoners. How did we claim this noble gesture as our own?

The bourgeoisie

Modern fencing is not egalitarian.

Though the aristocracy have dropped swords as their special privilege, swordplay is an haute bourgeois sport in France. Fencing was taken up chiefly by the moneyed classes in Australia, and it remains an elite game in the United States, Britain, and Western Europe. Alongside the costly equipment, the sport has typical high-status characteristics: individual not collective participation, formal not casual etiquette, light not heavy contact. The piste is not a football oval.

But this means fencing has become exactly what duelling was not: bourgeois. We are martial artists, but our class is more commercial than martial. The logic that originated in sixteenth-century Italy, and which helped to give rise to the duel — this logic has ended the duel.

Yes, officers of humble birth duelled in post-revolutionary France too, but they did so knowingly as gentlemen reaching for a gallant ideal. Now, the middle classes *are* the ideal. Vengeance for public slurs is taken in court, not with a court sword. Indeed, modern French libel law was written with duelling in mind, a way to make antagonism less bloody. Throughout Western Europe and its colonies, one can now save face by taking a foe's money, not their life — an ugly deal for any cavalier raised to loathe coin. 'We belong to a race amongst whom honour,' wrote French adventurer Émile Bruneau de Laborie, 'doesn't come with a price list.' (Bruneau de Laborie was bourgeois. He died in Africa from a lion bite.)

In keeping with the bourgeois ethos, swordplay is now a matter of middle-class institutions. On the piste or in the salle, there is no throng of nobles, united in strife by blood and divine grace. Instead, we have individuals coming together in abstract associations — typically with money and law between them. Here, life is often what Alasdair MacIntyre calls an 'arena': individuals fight for gain, shielded only by a few rights. German sociologist

Max Weber described this as the rationalisation of society: a shift from a logic of ethnicity, patronage, and kinship ('communalisation') to one of legality and economic transaction ('sociation').

Importantly, Weber called these ideas 'ideal types' or a 'utopia'. And perhaps Weber was not fair to the chivalric age, making it seem more monolithic than our own. But as intellectual lenses, his concepts help to focus on our civilisation's shift away from courtly rule to one of efficiency and calculability. It is Protestant austerity as a secular logic, ruled by what Weber called 'the technical and economic conditions of machine production'. Observe his language: instead of the more organic tropes of medieval life, we have the world as a giant mechanism in which people are parts.

Within this machine, our freely chosen games offer us what novelist and scholar J.R.R. Tolkien called a 'secondary world': a new universe, with its own roles and rules. As in duels, this little cosmos is codified. There are standardised rites, uniforms, and phrases. And this offers us a brief respite from those other games of capitalist society: family, schooling, career. But the stakes are not as high, thankfully. As we cross swords, we are only gambling with pride, not our lives.

My point is not that the middle classes are somehow alone in fantasy. Even duelling nobles had their own daydreams of ancient chivalry, which added lustre to their rusted armour. And I am not suggesting our bureaucratised world is less violent or more reasonable — it takes a great deal of force to enforce a 'free market', and many supposed rationalities produce ills. My point is simply that fencing has lost its nobility. As a sport, it is a bourgeois holiday from bourgeois reality.

Laughter or a shrug

In this, the fencing salute is a fascinating atavism.

During the age of duelling, to refuse an affair of honour was a death, of sorts — a social annihilation, in which one ceased to exist as a nobleman. (That is to say, to exist at all.) Regency gentleman Abraham Bosquet was in favour of laws against the grim custom. Yet he himself had duelled four times, believing that this tradition blunted vulgarity and sharpened politeness. More importantly, he knew that the beau monde shunned those who seemed craven. To flee from a challenge was to suffer 'the dreaded stigma of the censorious world'. A man might be coerced into apologising, but he thereby became polluted, a dirty man, transgressing society's basic categories. Cowardice as filth.

Yet a generation later, a challenge might be met with laughter or a shrug. Swords and guns were still available, as were hot-tempered officers to use them. But duelling was no longer a prestigious practice, no longer a seal of noble make. The basic culture of Britain — and later the rest of Europe — had shifted a little. That is to say, the world had changed. And in this world, a gentleman might be a little more sensitive, civil, and obedient to legislation — and still be a good gentleman. The concept of purity was widened to include men who wanted no blood on their hands.

The Czech novelist Milan Kundera once observed that Soviet rule in his country felt like it would last forever. There was no way beyond totalitarianism. He left for France to escape what he called 'the eternity of the Russian night'. And then the dawn rose: the Berlin Wall fell, Czechoslovakia had its Velvet Revolution, and what seemed endless was over in Kundera's own lifetime. From his novel, *Ignorance*:

> After the Russian invasion, since they had no inkling of Communism's eventual end, they ... believed they were inhabiting an infinity, and it was not the pain of their current life but the vacuity of the future that sucked dry their energies, stifled their courage, and made that ... twenty-year span so craven, so wretched.

And so it was with duelling. What seemed that most essential part of manhood was suddenly gone.

Put simply, our fencing salute is no longer Angelo's fencing salute. Yes, it is still a ritualised recognition, still a piece of etiquette that has lasted for centuries. And it has kept its bonds with ritualised mêlée. But the world behind this gesture has gone, and so the gesture has been transformed.

A little hand-waving

While the salute is no longer courtly, it is still courteous. We bourgeoisie have kept the formality suggested by the word, if not the full regal pomp.

As in the modern Japanese martial arts, the salute helps to civilise our violence. At its best, it suggests to you that I can be trusted, that I recognise you as a person and not *merely* as an object to be struck with an object. It also helps to remind me of this. It invites me to stop before the symbolic or literal bloodletting begins, and to witness the person before me.

The gesture is not a magical rite, transforming the training hall into a loving commune. Olympic fencing etiquette requires rules and punishments precisely because competitors are often so petty and rude. Morality cannot be forced, and certainly not with a little hand-waving.

Yet the gesture helps. Perhaps I am trying feverishly to smack you with a broadsword, as revenge for your last hit. Once again you struck my hand, and once again my thumb is swollen. But if I want to fence, I *must* salute you. And to do this, I must stay my vengeance for a moment. I must slow my martial rush and raise my sword to you, then sweep it down. And I must do this because I owe more to the institution than to my own pride or vanity. Put simply, this is bigger than I.

So, with the salute, we are trying to tie together loosely a fraying community. We have a culture already, but this culture is highly liberal, at least for its bourgeois beneficiaries. For all its gladiatorial force, our fencing school cannot wholly be this kind of arena. It cannot be held together with payments, state regulations, club rules — there must be more fundamental ethical ties.

The salute symbolises this process and, because we are symbolic beasts, is itself part of this process.

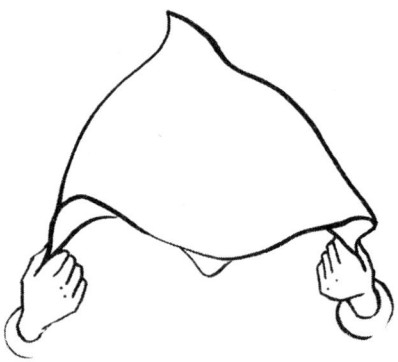

Hello There

Luke Skywalker lies stretched out: sandy hair on sand.

Raucous masked aliens ransack his car. Suddenly a silhouetted stranger appears, shouting and waving their hands. They wear a brown cowled robe, like a monk. The raiders flee, and the newcomer kneels beside the youth and touches his face. A small droid, watching from a niche in the cliff, cheeps and warbles with anxiety. Who is this anonymous stranger, dressed like a cleric? Will they beg Luke for alms? Hear his confession? Torture him with thumbscrews?

The stranger pulls back their hood gently with two hands.

Ah. It is an older man, his beard uncoloured and hair uncombed. We learn that this is Obi-Wan Kenobi, once a knight of the Jedi: an order of galactic warrior-clerics, who kept the peace for tens of thousands of years. 'Hello there,' he says to the droid with a very slight smile.

Hoods

In this way, the *Star Wars* hero meets his master — and so do we.

While Kenobi actor Alec Guinness was acutely responsive to gestures, his two-handed reveal has largely been snubbed by fandom in favour of his words (a grievous error). Yet filmmakers are keenly aware of the gesture. Ewan McGregor's younger Obi-Wan does it twice in subsequent films: once alongside his master Qui-Gon Jinn on a starship, and again alone as he comes in from the rain on an ocean planet. Each time, the same distinctive movements: both thumbs clasped on wool, the hood pulled back without haste.

No longer the whiny farm boy, Skywalker does this too. A full Jedi, he reveals himself to a slug-like criminal. His movements are deliberate and decisive now: he has grown up. He makes the same gesture after slicing and crushing troopers in a hallway. In a black habit like a Benedictine, he patiently slips his lightsaber to his belt to free his hands. Why? So he can very slowly — as if he were taking the wrapping off a holy relic — reveal himself. A lifetime later, he repeats the movement exactly. Standing on a cliff on a remote monastic island, he turns to us and uses two hands — one mechanical, one organic — to show his heroic face: beard uncoloured, hair uncombed. Perhaps his apprentice will eventually do the same.

So, generations of Jedi perform this same movement:

from Jinn to Kenobi, from Kenobi to Skywalker. Over at least six decades, republics rise and fall and rise — and so do large, floppy hoods.

Cinematic intimacy

This is obviously a filmic device, to raise suspense. Skywalker actor Mark Hamill acknowledges this technique. 'I just wanted to maximize the moment & heighten the inherent drama of the reveal,' he wrote, while also recognising the influence of Alec Guinness. The anonymity prompts tension, even when we believe we know the character: is this *really* him?

It is also a straightforward introduction. The face is typically seen as the most characteristic part of the corpus, what Ludwig Wittgenstein called the 'soul of the body'. This does not mean it is somehow more honest than the body. The face can deceive, as all actors know. Instead, its display is a phrase in the language of cinema. In *Raiders of the Lost Ark*, Indiana Jones steps into a shaft of jungle light after whipping a pistol from an assailant's hand: here is our no-nonsense hero. Shot only from behind, Héloïse in *Portrait of a Lady on Fire* walks quickly then sprints to the edge of high cliffs. Will she leap to escape her family, as her elder sister did? No, she turns to the camera for the first time, panting. She is exhilarated to simply run freely. Black marketeer Harry Lime is presumed dead in *The Third Man*. Then we find him suddenly illuminated on a Vienna street, puckish face lit from an apartment window. We get to know each person through their dramatic unveiling.

Likewise for Obi-Wan, whose face we see to finally

meet him properly — to encounter *him*, rather than merely his waving, wool-clad limbs.

This revelation has a moral atmosphere too. Few heroes keep their cowls or masks on, while villains often conceal themselves. Anakin Skywalker dons his hood after finally committing to his worst self. He eventually gets his iconic mask, as does his morally dubious grandson. A face we cannot see is suspicious, because it lacks both identity and the signs of fellow feeling. Put simply, Kenobi's revelation is a display of intimacy. The scruffy fellow is revealing that he can be trusted.

The Jedi is also revealing his mood: soothing, pacifying. In the medieval period when such cowls were common, hoods were used by all classes. They were worn while eating, sleeping, and worshipping; they were worn under open skies and ceilings alike. They were often only removed at leisure, and when comfortable or confident. In the fourteenth century, Chaucer poetised on this in his *Canterbury Tales*: a young man rides along merrily, his blond hair clad in only a cap 'for jolitee'. That is, to look handsome. The Jedi is not jaunty like this, but neither is he is stiff or awkward.

Put simply, Obi-Wan Kenobi is disclosed here as a man of personable ease. A man who has little to hide — and certainly not his face.

Authority

Yet witness how the Jedi's hood is pulled back. Not hurriedly, but calmly. Not aggressively, but gently. Not with one hand, but with two. This is a statement of formality and authority. Formal, because it is precise and very deliberate; authoritative, because it takes its time.

Kenobi is not casually jerking back his cowl, like a child in their cotton hoodie. There are no large, fast movements here: everything is just so. It suggests a primeval rite, as does its repetition by the Jedi over the generations. Sacred rituals offer up ancient beliefs, which arise again and again regardless of the aeons between. In fact, this is one of the hallmarks of rites — they seem to put the cosmos on pause.

As Pierre Bourdieu observes, being happy to take one's time is also a sign of power. It shows discipline, the cold blood of someone without worldly fever. Think of Aristotle's portrait of the great-souled man, a fully virtuous aristocrat:

> A slow step is thought proper to the proud man,
> a deep voice, and a level utterance; for the man
> who takes few things seriously is not likely to be
> hurried, nor the man who thinks nothing great
> to be excited, while a shrill voice and a rapid gait
> are the results of hurry and excitement.

This is from classical Athens, but it applies equally to the fictional galaxy. Obi-Wan Kenobi takes things seriously, but by staying aloof. The old monk does bold deeds with great-souled chill.

And he uses both hands to reveal himself as a sign of respect and seriousness. We often use two hands to lift what is weighty or protect what is fragile, and these metaphors guide thought and feeling. Literal heaviness becomes figurative heaviness. Kenobi's hood is light, but its existence matters symbolically: a double grip is called for.

So the Jedi is friendly with Luke, the kind uncle or

grandpa who understands the desert child. Yet he is no larking playmate, flying over Tattooine's dunes shooting womp rats. While seen as a mad hermit, this man has both status and sang-froid.

Monks

Kenobi is obviously wearing a hood to protect himself from the light of two suns. Tatooine is a dry desert, presumably with a thin atmosphere: no mist or fog between him and harsh solar radiation.

But the Jedi might also have worn a sombrero or pith helmet, might have sought simple practicality or regimental style among the dunes. Instead, he is dressed very much like a Franciscan in a brown cowled cloak. In short, this warrior elder looks like a medieval monk.

Monasticism was an institution of withdrawal from the world. And this was necessary because elite Christians believed this world was in decline. Of course, the world was always in decline for those who found ordinary life ugly and evil. Since the exile from Eden, it was fallen: a series of sins and temptations to sin. Witness Pietro Damiani, an eleventh-century Benedictine monk. Against travel, scholarship, polite conversation, comfortable clothes, he counselled a war against secular life:

> Dearest brothers, seize the arms of all the virtues
> — sobriety, humility, patience, obedience,
> chastity, charity — and fight not on behalf of
> your fields or cities, not for your children or
> wives, but for your souls which rise above every
> emotion of relationship.

Most monks were not so frothing-at-the-mouth hermetic. Instead, they were a new scholarly elite. Monasticism began partly because Christendom was losing Rome's academic, legal, and governmental institutions. These centuries were not simply dark ages, merely waiting for the Renaissance's illumination. They were lively, innovative, and highly pluralistic. But they no longer offered the training that Rome guaranteed. Alongside food and board, monasteries offered liturgy, literacy, and bureaucracy. Whatever happened in courts and on battlefields, these frocked men could read and write, pray and sing. Monks were often encouraged to live saintly lives in a supposedly devilish world. They fled to their rooms or common tables, then returned to the world resanctified — or at least rejuvenated.

In this way, the monks saw themselves as custodians of a dying civilisation. Or rather, they were ardent Christians in an apathetically Christian world. Or rather, they held on to those fragments of the classical era that their forebears did not burn, chisel away, or print over.

To continue these ancient ways, the monks had to be disciplined. While they typically avoided peasant labour, their lives were strict, austere, and highly formalised. They were living a heightened rationality, what sociologist Max Weber called 'the supremacy of a purposeful will'. (A will that later became capitalistic.) While their clothing was supposed to be simple, it also symbolised this power. In keeping with Damiani's idea of a grand spiritual battle, the monks' habits suggested holy virility. They might have been celibate scribes and singers, but they were manly in their piety.

This is what Kenobi suggests in his cowled robe: the genius of the collapsed republic, kept alive within him. This is also what he suggests with his quiet, careful movements: the esoteric wisdom of someone trained by a cultish regimen.

Not monks

Yet the Jedi are not Christian monks, despite the obvious nods to them. The Jedi are also not samurai, despite borrowing liberally from Japanese cinema and ideas. The word 'Jedi' itself comes from 'jidaigeki' (period films), and George Lucas' debt to director Akira Kurosawa is well known. Kenobi is basically wearing a kimono under his European cloak, while his Jedi philosophy is often Buddhism lite. The idea is not to reflect actual theology or philosophy, but to suggest that the older man is a 'monk and samurai warrior ... a sort of medieval elder or priest'.

Kenobi's habit and manner are akin to a tourist's monasticism, more style than lived substance, more a vague screen upon which fantasies of serenity can be projected. This is also why the Jedi can be many things to many fans. Some see them as Stoics, seeking principled calm instead of surrendering to rage or lust. Others see them as Kierkegaardian, leaping into the seeming absurdity of faith. Lucas quite deliberately kept things 'roomy', as one biographer put it tactfully. This approach suggested as much as possible to as many audiences as possible, without the demands of scholarship or spirituality. It is a cinematic aesthetic, not a way of life.

Yes, the Jedi code has become an ethos for some moderns, who see it as a philosophy or even a religion. Some are knowingly turning these films into a lifestyle, fully aware that the scripts have no grand metaphysical or ethical vision. They do not want to *be* Jedi, they simply want a more modern mythos for their spiritual rites. Alex Bird, from the Temple of the Jedi Order: 'Yoda's a puppet, we all know he's a puppet. But we've come to another conclusion and it is this: that myths are true, all myths are true. Not literally true; they're truths about us, they're stories about us, they're always stories about people.' This is a surprisingly consistent way of living.

But the Jedi themselves do not suggest life. They are like action figures snapped together from a large pile of broken bits. Obi-Wan is not a historical monk, Eastern or Western — he is the suggestion of a monk, living in a fictional Middle Ages of 'elementary and outlaw feelings', as Umberto Eco put it. Kenobi stands in for a vague idea of ancient and austere wisdom amid the ruins. His gesture is supposed to evoke the weight of monastic knowledge and ritual, without those extra burdens of fact.

Thentasy

This is Hollywood nostalgia.

For much of its history, 'nostalgia' was a medical term. Invented in the seventeenth century, it referred to homesick soldiers. In this era, Swiss mercenaries were known to suffer fever, stomach-aches, fainting fits, and even death — all for love of their lost Alps, with their herdsman's songs. This malaise was familiar to many ancient exiles, from Odysseus to Ovid ('I am oppressed by skies in which all constellations bode ill'), but the Enlightenment diagnosis was new.

While the diagnosis changed over the years, this

idea of nostalgia continued until well into the twentieth century. Then nostalgia suddenly became less a physician's observation and more a cultural critic's slur: of sentimental longing for yesteryear.

Importantly, nostalgia has always actually been a yearning for both space *and* time. Because we always exist through each of these, the loss of home means some loss of ourselves. But as a popular word, nostalgia now has little to do with aching for Helvetica's mountains, Ithaca's rugged hills, or Rome's stars. It is a wistful backward glance, a teary smile over one's shoulder.

I call this 'thentasy': the fantasy of then. And this gaze comes in two kinds, biographical and historical.

The first is typically a fondness for youth. Instead of the pains of adulthood, I chase the pleasures of childhood. I seek in yesterday what I no longer have today: excitement, laughter, hope. Psychologists argue that this yearning can be beneficial, allowing me to be ambivalent during stress. Yes, I rightly feel sadness or fear, because life is painful. But I can also feel some joy, thinking of what I once had. It was true and good. This kind of thentasy might leave me more nimble mentally, less hamstrung by my own moods. It can reportedly help with loneliness, nearing death, and absurdity, though perhaps not for those with no cherished childhood to turn towards. Biographical thentasy suggests that life (still) has meaning, drawing on the best of what was to help us cope with what will be.

Historical thentasy is typically less healthy. I pine for the good old days, which are good precisely because they were old — and I was not alive to witness them. Think of someone sighing over soirées in colonial finery or marching for their once-glorious empire. Each picture conveniently omits the sordid privation and violence, leaving the nostalgic with only rueful happiness or righteous fury.

In short, historical thentasy works precisely because it is not historiography. It is not an earnest grapple with the past, aware of its slipperiness. It is a flattering, comforting, or merely amusing show. As historian David Lowenthal puts it: 'it is the feeling of pastness that counts'. Yes, this can be playfully ironic, knowingly toying with a past that is long passed. But historical nostalgia chiefly describes a painless 'then', which offers the balm of exotic familiarity. There is enough difference here to entertain, but not enough to discomfit.

In this light, *Star Wars* is doubly nostalgic. It takes the ingredients of the creator's childhood — dogfight scenes, Flash Gordon and cowboy serials, John Carter of Mars, *Casablanca*, and so on — and makes a sweet dessert. Lucas himself put it this way: 'It's all the things that are great put together. It's not like one kind of ice cream but rather a very big sundae.' The Jedi are as much about twentieth-century pop culture as they are about spirituality and martial valour. And a generation on, the original films and prequels are now themselves works of thentasy. The sequels look back at their own franchise confectionary with a glutted smile.

Alongside this biographical candy is sugared-coated history: medieval Christianity, republican Rome, feudal Japan. It offers nothing sophisticated or sublime like Umberto Eco's *The Name of the Rose*, Marguerite Yourcenar's *Memoirs of Hadrian*, or Shūsaku Endō's *Silence*. Lucas' universe is a benign mélange of eras, used for their style more than their substance. In a franchise known for its special effects, history too is a special effect.

It adds worldly authenticity to a very simple American story of heroic triumph.

The problem here is not that the *Star Wars* universe is false. Make-believe has its own autonomy, which does not simply answer to established fact. As John Dewey put it: 'no genuine work has ever been a repetition of anything that previously existed.' Fiction arises within history, but it cannot *be* history. Entertainment is not a thesis.

The problem with Lucas' *Star Wars* is that it is simplistic, vague, and calculated for sales rather than poignancy. The hermit's religious gesture of revelation promises so much more than it can provide.

Oneness

George Lucas has freely acknowledged his debt to Joseph Campbell, popular mythophile. Campbell offered the director a basic recipe for Skywalker's journey: the 'monomyth', which supposedly lies beneath heroic stories of all cultures.

In this vision, Obi-Wan Kenobi is an existential and cosmic guide. He beckons the hero to leave his old life and keeps him safe as he enters the new. A wizard or hermit who helps the hero become what he *must* be, the guide is a symbol of breadth and depth. 'What such a figure represents,' Campbell wrote, 'is the benign, protecting power of destiny. The fantasy is a reassurance — a promise that the peace of Paradise, which was known first within the mother womb, is not to be lost.'

Campbell was an antisemitic reactionary whose dubious legacy is rarely recognised. Not surprisingly, he was a fiend for the hazy, hoary oneness so loved by Blackshirts. One nation, one blood, one aesthetic — all ancient and eternal. Scepticism is warranted here. Still, Campbell saw rightly that Tatooine's 'crazy old man' Kenobi is more than a teacher, ally, or friend. He stands in for a better world, in which the future eventually gains the supposed concord of the past. Campbell flavoured his ideal with sickly fascist mythology, Lucas with more palatable American liberalism for children (then sold us toys). Neither was overly concerned with the actual stuff of history.

When he pulls back his cowl, Obi-Wan Kenobi reveals the face of this yesteryear: vague unity, offered with a benign smile.

Aiki

As students, my friend and I philosophised together. (We were not friends. We were friendly.)

We were in a café between a soon-to-be-bankrupt clothing store and a soon-to-be-sold lingerie boutique. We sat between the window and the soon-to-be-passé focaccia.

We discussed the universe in highly abstract ways: is it pure change or eternal stillness? Is it basically vague or does it welcome measurement? I was a student of process philosophy, seeking dynamism and connectedness. He was a student of physics, concerned chiefly with fixity and division.

I quoted Heraclitus at my friend: 'all things are in motion and nothing is at rest'. This bothered him, which pleased me. Perhaps he had that ancient fear of change and multiplicity, of existence as riptide and maelstrom.

Running a slender hand through his grey hair, he replied with the ease of a man for whom the world is simply everything that is the case. He said that the universe is a mathematical continuum. Like a commercial block, the cosmos can always be divided into more lots. He dropped a wiry grid onto reality: a comforting, consoling grid.

Not yet ...

I asked whether these lots can be divided into more lots, and those divided in turn, and so on — a cosmic realtor's perverse fantasy. My friend agreed with a slow, cautious nod. He was wary.

Now.

I used my riddle. Suppose I want to walk from the expensive lingerie store to the expensive urban wear store — how can I? To do this, I must first walk half-way between the lots. Yet before I can walk half-way, I must first walk a quarter of the way. And so on. Logically, it is not possible for me to arrive, since there is a never-ending series of waypoints that must be crossed before I can get to the next. I can never spend my scholarship money on artfully pre-torn jeans. In fact, I can never even leave my chair beside the window, as all movement involves the same fractions of fractions.

This was not my own puzzle, but one of Zeno of Elea's paradoxes given a modern polish. In the fifth-century before the common era, Zeno said that motion simply cannot exist, because 'that which is in locomotion must arrive at the half-way stage before it arrives at the goal'. An impish conundrum, but a conundrum nonetheless.

I grinned, suspecting he had no answer. (I also had no

answer, but I wanted to give *him* pause.)

He began to reply, looked down at his lap, sipped his now-cold black coffee. Then he stopped and stared. With Zeno, I had trapped him within his own cosmos, made a snare of his grid of wires. Put simply, I had turned his attack against him and gained my victory.

As I conquered my friend, I did something curious with my hands, something even more obscure than this obscure conversation. I swept my upturned right palm from left to right, then curled it as if grasping. Then I pulled back this hand while jabbing my left towards him.

Forms

These movements were from a karate kata.

In the Japanese martial arts, kata are sequences of techniques. They are performed solo, but there is little spontaneity: the movements are standardised and refined. The horse stance must be just so low, the kick's toes just so pointed, the breathing just so timed. Anthropologist Rupert Cox compares kata to the tea ceremony: 'There is rarely a moment when the body is not trying to adjust itself so as to accommodate all the details of correct form.'

Kata can be sublime to watch. The varied cadence of slow parries or fast punches; the snap of starched cotton uniforms; the athleticism of lunges or leaps — these suggest powerful forces, but on a human scale. Kata are also thrilling to perform, even when the performer cannot see them. Philosopher Markus Schrenk calls this a 'proprioceptive art': enjoyed from the inside rather than from the outside. Because of this, kata can be more beautiful for the doer than for the seer.

Kata are meditative, encouraging a focused yet abstract state of mind, a mood in which concentration expands while selfhood shrinks. Japanese martial artists describe this as a consciousness that is nowhere, empty, or nothing, while psychologist Mihaly Csikszentmihalyi calls it 'flow'. These states arise differently in different cultures, yet the basic psychophysiology is the same. Striving skilfully in a challenging practice leaves us feeling blissfully at one with this practice. Gōgen Yamaguchi, grandmaster of the Gōjū-ryū style of karate, spoke of this as 'a state of nothingness ... freed to act without interruption or thought'.

Beyond beauty and reverie, kata also have a more utilitarian role: aides-mémoires. What became karate-dō was first developed in villages. Forms were demonstrated by teachers, then performed and corrected, performed and corrected, performed and corrected. 'Practice should be done ten, twenty, fifty, a hundred times without stopping,' wrote master Shigeru Egami. 'You must practice until your body understands.' These movements were then interpreted for their tactics and strategies. In this way, kata were guidebooks for oral societies, what Goshi Yamaguchi calls 'a technical training textbook'. Europe also used solo drills centuries ago, though they were often described in books for literate aristocrats. In karate, instruction manuals were written chiefly through the body.

This is why I remembered parts of a kata in a café, over a decade after learning it; why I still remember these parts today, many years and kilometres from that steamy mirrored room. For a century, the form has endured from teacher to student, teacher to student — and finally to me.

Agōn

So, while arguing over coffee, my hands were making fighting moves. This is not surprising, since I then practised philosophy as kind of combat.

My vocation is defined variously — in fact, defining philosophy is itself part of philosophy. Put another way, its existence is always up for grabs. Philosophers think differently and write differently, and our stylistic choices are not merely decorative: they arise from some basic way of life.

But whether philosophy is known sentimentally as 'the love of wisdom' or more carefully as Whitehead's 'critic of abstractions', it has a history of conflict. Argument becomes competition. Nietzsche argued that this was why that ugly satyr Socrates was so appealing to handsome Athenian nobles. He made thinking like grappling or boxing. This was what the Greeks called 'agōn': contest or struggle. It is no coincidence that 'Plato' was perhaps a wrestling nickname from the Greek for 'broad' — it suggested the lad's 'robust figure' from exercise. Plato was the perfect aristocrat for this new game.

Many centuries later, the typically peaceable Scot David Hume also described his philosophy as an invasion of scholarship:

> instead of taking now and then a castle or village
> on the frontier [we may] march up directly to
> the capital or center of these sciences, to human
> nature itself; which being once masters of, we
> may every where else hope for an easy victory.
> From this station we may extend our conquests
> over all those sciences ...

For all its daydreams of civilised talk, philosophy has kept this agonistic bent, this interest in winning. We talk of attacking and defending ideas, of claiming or losing territory, of practising logical jūjutsu.

When I brought out my puzzle in that café, this was not a generous offering, a boon, motivated by kindness. It was a tactic in my strategy of conquest. I wanted to win, and my hands played along.

Seiyunchin

Amid the thump of digital bass and hiss of steaming milk, I was performing part of a kata called Seiyunchin.

Translations of this name vary from the prosaic ('set of pushing and pulling') to the poetic ('blue hawk fight'.) For me, Seiyunchin has always been grabby and poky. Someone punches me, I parry with my right hand. Then I grip their wrist, jerk them down and towards me. This leaves their side open. Still holding their arm, I spear-hand them in the kidneys.

So, what seemingly continued from Japan to the Australian suburbs were four techniques: block, grab, pull, strike. These were less about beauty and meditation, and more about beating an intellectual foe: overcoming my friend with his own efforts.

This principle is sometimes called 'aiki' in Japanese, and is described in jūdō as 'the art of giving way'. It involves not only guiding an enemy's momentum, but also welcoming this without panic or rage. An early twentieth-century textbook describes aiki simply as 'an impassive state of mind': not because it is lethargic or meek, but because it involves allowing an aggressor to act savagely against us. This general approach pervades the Japanese martial arts, from the older jūjutsu, to modern kendō and karate-dō.

Not coincidentally, I was using a version of this logic in the café. I let my friend mount his intellectual attack on my Heraclitean concept, allowed him to introduce his continuum model of the universe. Then I grabbed this concept and trapped it with Zeno's reductio ad absurdum, or argument to the 'impossible'. Used by Socrates in Plato's works, this involves accepting an antagonist's premises then showing how they lead to absurdity — or what seems like absurdity to the antagonist.

The reductio ad absurdum is not a conclusive triumph but is certainly a fine coup. It takes a seemingly strong position and reveals its weaknesses. And part of its success comes from its stance of approval: what looks like agreement becomes ridicule. At the very least, this is a cunning rhetorical ploy, which weakens confidence. The adversary's strongest movement is turned against them.

In this light, Hellenic Zeno and the Japanese blue hawk fight are not worlds apart, historically or geographically. The puzzle and the hand techniques followed a similar logic: accept, redirect, incapacitate.

Seal, stamp, mark

My kata movements signified my control over my opponent. They also signified my control over myself.

As I blocked and grabbed and jabbed, this was an incantation of sorts. I felt more sure of myself, more brave, more clever. For want of a better word, I felt more *real*.

The so-called 'traditional' martial arts are certainly

known to increase young people's confidence, regardless of the styles' martial value. For me, this increase was expressed literally with smug hand-waving. Had these Seiyunchin movements been a verbal language, their meaning would have been closer to a prayer than to a propositional statement — an outpouring and upraising of belief.

This is no coincidence. The Japanese martial arts have a strong ritual element. Ceremonial gestures are common in Buddhism and Daoism, which influenced combat philosophy and custom. Think of statues of the Buddha with his right palm up, left palm facing up on his lap: this is semui-in, which suggests fearlessness. The word 'in' here means a seal, mark, or sign. So hand movements symbolise doctrine and divinity, but also authenticity, much like a wax stamp on a document. They make certain themes visible, tangible — and *veritable*.

Signs of doctrine but also of magic, these were taken up by combative communities. They were a feature of medieval Japanese fiction, with one warrior escaping from his enemies by conjuring sorcerous mist with his hands. They appeared in some of Japan's older koryū martial arts, and what is dubiously called 'ninjutsu' today. The modern kata I learned in Gōjū-ryū karate-dō included strikingly similar gesticulations.

These gestures serve several roles in fighting arts: martial, religious, and meditative. Yes, I can parry with my palm, seemingly knocking away a reverse punch. But in the same movements, I can partake in a rite that suggests stories of bravery or enlightenment. In this way, I myself become a scriptural character of sorts, a Buddha or Manjushri, palm or sword-hand held high. My ego firms up with my fist. (Not a very Buddhist therapy.)

My point is not that these martial arts can be reduced to icons or rituals. Combat is a mongrel institution, with no one reason for snapping or howling. My point is that, when those Seiyunchin movements guided my mood, this was no modern novelty. Fighting has always been a semiotic as well as a physical pursuit, and often its performances alter ourselves rather than our enemies.

David Hume once observed that a belief is simply an idea we feel strongly about. 'An idea assented to feels different from a fictitious idea,' he wrote, 'and this different feeling I endeavour to explain by calling it a superior force.' In this sense, I used those karate-dō techniques to feel very strongly about karate *and* about myself. In the dōjō and the suburban café, I waved my hands and lent myself this superior force.

So, this was defence of the self, though existentially not physically. To change metaphors, I was stamping an ancient seal upon my own character. ('Character', from the ancient Greek: mark, brand, engraving.)

Weakness

I thought I was part of some ancient purity.

The founder of Gōjū-ryū karate, Chōjun Miyagi, taught kata to his student, Gōgen Yamaguchi. Yamaguchi taught his student. His student taught me. From Japan to Australia, I continued a century of authentic karate-dō. I developed a unique Oriental art, and I later used this art to convey and bolster my intellectual arts. The beneficiary of centuries of secret wisdom, my karate was strong, perfect, and original.

Yes, this is a neat story — and wholly false.

To begin, my spear-hand was actually an illusion, more chimera than coup de grâce. It would have ended with phalangeal fractures. Yes, Okinawan martial artists were known to condition their hands by shoving them into sand, slowly toughening their skin, muscles, and perhaps bones. Sand was then replaced with pebbles, and perhaps pebbles with rocks. Others used bundles of bamboo, shoving and gripping between the sticks. These led to tales of brawn, like the great founder ripping strips of flesh off beef with only his fingers, or crushing bamboo.

Putting aside the truth of these legends, my hands were neither hardened nor strengthened. I had not sunk my fingers in sand since kindergarten — they were for typing, not stabbing.

This mistake was part of a more general error: I believed my karate-dō made me almost magically secure. I certainly defended myself in several fights, and I write 'defended' quite deliberately: I protected myself, and little more. But having now encountered everything from boxing and European fencing to Muay Thai and Brazilian jujutsu, I realise I was enjoying an arrogant fantasy. There are countless combatants who could wound or kill me with little more than a punch, thrust, or choke.

I was more ego than fists.

Not pure, not original

My failures were also intellectual. I was quite wrong about Seiyunchin itself, believing it some original Japanese secret, and that I was a pious seeker of unique lore.

Even within Gōjū-ryū, there are several versions of these kata, and several interpretations of each. In one school, my block might indeed be a parry, which becomes a pull and strike to the ribs. Or it might be a double armlock, a neck hold, then an eye gouge. Or it might be a parry, after which the head is jerked down and struck. There might be a little wrist lock while pulling the arm; there might not.

So, what I thought of as *the* four Seiyunchin movements were actually a handful of choices among so many others.

More importantly, these ideas occur in martial arts all over the world. They are practiced in Korean taekwondo, using a hooking block and spear-hand. In Choy Li Fut kung fu from southern China, they are 'palm facing bridge', 'latching-on bridge', and 'pointing fingers' or 'arrow fingers'. And the very same principle of aiki continues where the techniques do not. My café movements might have been familiar to fighters across the centuries and continents.

This is partly common physiology. Whether we use a fist, foot, or sword, our attacks are vulnerable in this way. As soon as our lead limb is before us, it can be turned across us, leaving our torso and back open. Martially, this is an invitation to punch or kick our kidneys or slip a blade between our ribs. If we have this particular physiology, we will have this particular weakness.

But the martial arts are not merely mechanical enterprises, not simply calculations of forces, vectors, stress. They are also social enterprises, and their development is as much cultural as physiological.

And the culture of karate-dō is not entirely Japanese. Yes, many of its popular tropes are Japanese innovations. But it came from the island of Okinawa, where martial arts were often simply called 'te' or 'ti': hand. And for most of its history, Okinawa was not part of Japan. It was its own sovereign nation.

There, the combat arts were practised more casually, and named after villages like Naha-te and Shuri-te. These were not official organisations, but local communities. A generation after Japan annexed Okinawa, karate became mass physical education for mainland students. As part of a nationalistic push to develop Japanese education in the Meiji era, these practices were transformed from island fighting arts to imperial disciplinary and spiritual pursuits. The pupils were now the supposed heirs to bushidō, the samurai code of duty and etiquette. This propaganda helped the Japanese welcome what was otherwise seen as foreign thuggery for peasants.

The point is not that te was actually brutish scrapping or karate a fascist lie. Okinawan fighting had its own graces and reveries, and some older Japanese values and ideals do indeed continue in karate today. But karate-dō did not magically arise from the divine genius of a few Japanese founders, and as a modern art it is far less traditional than its advertising suggests.

Okinawan hand was not wholly an Okinawan invention either. Over the centuries, the island was part of a large economic and cultural exchange that included Japan and China, alongside Korea, Indonesia, the Philippines, and India. The founder of Gōjū-ryū was taught by the local Naha-te master Kanryō Higaonna. And who schooled Higaonna? Perhaps a mysterious fighter called Ryū Ryū Ko or Xie Ru Ru, who taught Higaonna in southern China.

In other words, Higaonna learned kung fu, as did his student Miyagi. Karate began in China, where arts like Fujian White Crane supposedly grew out of the famous Shaolin temple. Like karate-dō, these were as much therapeutic and spiritual exercises as combat skills, and arose within the late Ming and early Qing dynasties. Not surprisingly, a very similar parry, grab, and punch occurs in at least one description of Shaolin boxing.

My ego-firming palm symbols also occurred outside Japan. From the Sanskrit for 'seal', mudras appeared in Indian martial arts, including kaḷaripayaṭṭu. In China, Daoists and Buddhists both developed hand signals, and both influenced the Shaolin: their staff and empty-hand arts respectively. The temple's fighters called upon their tutelary deity's powers with 'palm signs and oral spells'.

Japanese nationalists were quick to downplay this foreign guidance, just as Koreans later did to the Japanese. The kanji characters for karate-dō originally meant 'Tang martial arts', after the Chinese dynasty. They became the homophonous 'empty hand' and China's chalk was wiped from the educational blackboard.

So, well over three centuries before I learned Seiyunchin in a fluorescent-lit school behind a provincial car park, martial artists were practising something like aiki. Many were also performing meditative rites with their hands, enchanting themselves if not their enemies. My proud lineage — originator, to grandmaster, to master, to teacher, to me — offered no guarantees of purity or originality.

I turned a mixed genealogy into a falsely pure essence.

Orientalism

I did not pick up this mythos from the dōjō, or training hall.

The dōjō has its own illusions and shibboleths, of

course: this unbeatable strike, that unbreakable skin, those untested and unquestioned pronouncements. In the modern Japanese martial arts, masters' authority and students' credulity often trump realism. But my teacher was typically down to earth, preferring the simple and practical to the esoteric.

No, these falsehoods existed well before I ever stepped barefoot on the mats. As a child, Japan seemed a land of timeless and peerless knowledge, where masters killed with a single punch. This was not merely technical knowledge, though; not like classes at school. This was an arcanum of spiritual transcendence, passed on by superhuman foreigners. Better still, the Japanese promised a kind of moralised combat. To become a better karateka was to become a better human being, and vice versa. If life in Melbourne was humdrum, karate promised a more enchanted cosmos: beautiful, exciting, and blessed by the serenity of the magically dangerous.

The point is not simply that I was wrong about karate-dō and Japan — although I was. The point is that my illusions were off the shelf, not bespoke. They existed well before I wore bleached canvas and tried to crack coconuts with my palm.

Like China and India, Japan was seen by many Europeans as an exotic other. While our caricatures of the East were often of bestial savages or effete slaves, they were not all mocking or vilifying. For some, Asia in general and Japan in particular stood for something the West had lost, some hallowed wisdom, primordial and pristine. This was a flattering version of the idea that the Orient was a civilisation in decline, regressive where ours was progressive. Literary scholar Edward Said famously called this 'Orientalism'. For Said, colonialism and scholarship worked together to invent a 'Platonic essence' of a people or peoples. This was distilled by and for occupying powers, providing them with a known and exploitable tonic.

Said's ideas about the Levant cannot be applied thoughtlessly to Japan. Most obviously, this nation was itself a coloniser. The Japanese invented lowly personas for the countries they invaded, like Korea. Despite their bad-faith denials, they have a history of xenophobic policies and bigoted ideas, chiefly against minorities and their Asian neighbours. This country is no meek, innocent victim of European imperialism.

Also, European scholars' ideas of Japan varied historically, ranging from stock caricatures of the 'Asiatic' to nuanced celebrations of autonomy and dignity. And where westerners were wrong about the nation, this was sometimes because of sloppy, partial, or mercenary scholarship, not merely because of colonialism.

Still, there was certainly a tradition of Anglophone culture that was straightforwardly Orientalist. This depicted Japan as a primitive land of antiquity, full of mysterious warriors, proud tyranny, and aesthetic finery — though ultimately lacking in Western rationality and innovation. And some of those who held up this vision — including Ruth Benedict, who wrote the bestselling *The Chrysanthemum and the Sword* — were scholars who spoke no Japanese, and had never even visited the country.

Many Japanese took this fantasy as their own. It was often encouraged by those conservatives who most benefited from the illusion. It is no coincidence that karate, once Okinawan, was consecrated as bushidō right after Japan's humiliating defeat by the Allies. As the Japanese had occupied Okinawa, so the Allies now occupied Japan. Modern budō martial arts were a way to recover and rejuvenate nihonjinron: Japaneseness. While the Americans were replacing those in power with fascists and nationalists, Japanese conservatives were tweaking their national identity. Many of the English-speaking victors took this vision home with them, creating what scholar Kevin Tan calls 'a growing commercialised Oriental martial mythology'.

And this is the mythos I found in Melbourne's provincial suburbs. Or rather, that found me.

I spoke no Japanese until high school, and had never visited Japan. In fact, I had never met anyone from Japan until I began training in karate. Yet I just *knew* this nation of ninja and samurai would teach me lessons unavailable in ordinary Melbourne, and unimagined by us gaijin. I gained this certainty from movies, television, comics, video games; from stories of meek yet fearsome Eastern masters coming to the West, or virtuous white boys taught or raised by Orientals. Watching *Bloodsport* taught me about the 'death touch', and *Pray for Death* the Japanese warrior's devotion to family and vengeance. In the comic *Wolverine*, I witnessed modern Japan full of katana duels, 'pressure point' strikes, and tragedies of honour and filial piety. Playing the computer game *Budokan*, I smacked my foes with nunchakus before rice-paper screens and a tranquil Shintō shrine. Japan had the world's swiftest swords, most clandestine assassins, most deadly fists — and all so uniquely attractive.

And all of this was behind my hands years later, as I parried and thrust over an espresso.

Not wanting to know

How did I fail to know this?

Chiefly because I did not *want* to know, because it suited me to be a fantasist. With my black belt and purple knuckles, I felt so much better about myself. This was not simply because karate-dō was an atavistic and supreme art, but because I believed I was worthy of this art. I was flattering myself morally as well as martially.

This is no great surprise. As Plato had Socrates observe, we like to think of ourselves as good — or at least seeking the good. This is not merely a truism. To be moral is not simply to recite cant or behave obediently, it is to genuinely want what is best. We have longings for something lacking, and that something is better than we are.

But in order to gain this something, we have to know exactly what is best. Often we do not. We do not see clearly because clarity hurts. Platonist Iris Murdoch once called consciousness 'a cloud of more or less fantastic reverie designed to protect the psyche from pain', and this mist is so very comfortable. It is easy to earnestly devote ourselves to something beautiful — and for this beauty to be misleading and misguiding. We can be perfectly certain that our ideals are the only ones. We alone recognise the verity in a lunge and elbow. We alone seek high wisdom while others seek only common savagery. *Of course* I believed I was a righteous warrior-sage, questing after truth.

So, I was ignorant — but not merely ignorant. I deployed my ignorance with care. I did not leave my cluelessness to chance. This was one of Jean-Paul Sartre's better observations: repression requires knowledge. In order to steadfastly avoid knowing something, I have to be aware of it.

This is why I dismissed criticisms of karate-dō from Anglophones or Chinese as racism against the Japanese, why I trivialised gibes from sporting fighters as a mania for medals over honourable combat. And when critics were obviously right about karate, I said they were not talking about *real* karate — not the ancient genius of Gōjū-ryū, handed from master to student, master to student, master to me. They were merely observing mall fighting, the sad consequences of Western European capitalist commodification.

Here, I was parrying attacks with the confident agility of someone trained in intellectual fisticuffs — shadow-boxing against doubt itself. And I was doing it to keep myself away from the good and the true.

Social illusions

One way to safeguard falsehood is to seek help. So I chose like-minded friends and acquaintances. I spoke to an aikidōka about ki or vital energy, and a jūdōka about falling safely. I bickered with a Shitō-ryū student about the aesthetics of our respective kata, and with another Gōjū-ryū student about the best canvas in uniforms. I was continually reflecting, analysing, speculating like a good little philosopher. Yet at no point did I move beyond our shared doxa: the obvious, taken-for-granted world, with its limits about what can be thought, said, and done. Bourdieu called doxa 'the universe of the undiscussed', and I remained happily within my cosmos. I kept my hands over my mouth, like Iwazaru the monkey.

This is why philosophy must be a gregarious pursuit, because even the most radically doubting Cartesian will have even more radical prejudices. We require others to highlight our unspoken, unnoticed notions.

We cannot avoid prejudices — we *are* our prejudices. We always have some sense of how the world exists, and what it means for anything to exist at all. An enlightened life means revealing and recognising our assumptions, not pretending to live without them.

And one way to achieve this is by encountering the other, by allowing our horizons and theirs to come together. By seeking foreign people or peoples, we can become more aware of what we ourselves take for granted — including what we mean by 'foreign' and 'ourselves'.

Plato the oiled-up wrestler recognised something of this. While he praised the student who could 'reason soberly by himself', his dialogues celebrated the idea that moral growth only happened intimately, alongside others who were also seeking betterment. If philosophy was a purely solitary activity, Socrates would not have needed to be the 'midwife' of others' ideas. His conversations were not simply theories, abstract and universal. They were themselves exercises in education, as Socrates offered each the lessons they needed. Put simply, Plato did not merely write about ethical development — he portrayed it artfully, and he took great pains to include the living milieu of Athens in his portrayal.

As a karateka, I needed more of this social conflict. I ought to have sought, not simply a more honest consciousness, but a more honest community — a fraternity of truth-seekers who did not share my convictions about Seiyunchin's sorcerous powers.

This is exactly what I did *not* do. Instead of allowing

my horizons to make one another more unambiguous and understandable, I kept them apart. The ordinary world of everyday Australia and the supernatural world of Japan. The ugly and the beautiful. The mortal and the superhuman. The vulgar and the cultivated.

As a philosopher, I made caricatures of both civilisations by always seeking those who held the same stereotypes sacred.

It takes a village to raise — a fantasy.

On worlds

Which brings me back to that café, with its trip-hop loops and philosophical chat.

On that afternoon, I was arguing about worlds in the most abstract ways: their movement or stillness, messiness or neatness. Fancies of ultimate truths. The whole universe was mine to describe metaphysically — that is to say, to claim as my intellectual territory. And as I attacked my friend's defences, I waved my hands suitably.

As I performed my Seiyunchin rite, I did not realise that there was another cosmos surrounding me. I spoke of transience, but not of the changes that took the kata's techniques from China to Okinawa to Japan to suburban Australia. I knew of process philosophy, but not the actual processes that translated Buddhist and Daoist customs from temples into classes behind a provincial car park. I spoke of forces, yes. But not those of colonialism and Orientalism, not those of magical thinking and the macho denial of vulnerability.

Put simply, I was talking about the world as if I were

an observer, someone lucky enough to watch the cosmos from beyond. But I was very much in the world, and I carried it with me in every block, grab, and strike.

There is an irony in this. Seiyunchin's principle of aiki is straightforward: taking an opponent's force and turning it against them. What seems like dominating strength becomes submissive weakness; the yielding hand is eventually controlling.

This logic is also at work here in history. Or rather, at the point where history meets biography.

When the Japanese took Okinawan arts, they continued a legacy. It was changed, of course, but was a legacy nonetheless. In doing so, they allowed generations of Japanese children to be taught island fighting — children who now laud this heritage as elders. And likewise for Allied soldiers and civilians who sent their kids into gymnasiums wearing baggy bright white, to be taught by these Japanese elders or their students. I have devoted years to karate-dō, which also involves movements from other colonial states: nineteenth-century Okinawa, seventeenth-century China, perhaps classical India. Now I am part of their legacy too.

This is a troubling analogy, which too easily becomes a glib excuse for colonialism: the thief, crying that stolen rings are stuck on his fingers. I am not excusing violent pillage. I am simply noting that part of these cultures is now literally within me, and doubly so: as an axiom of combat, but also as the very principle that gave me this axiom.

Japan yielded, and eventually controlled my hands. Aiki.

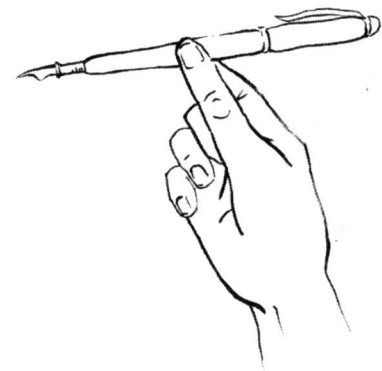

Catching the Light

Yet another café.

This one is a tiny bar with baroque furniture alongside a wide, high atrium. Five or six storeys of red brick. Sitting under the skylight with my black coffee, I am enjoying that midwinter novelty: warmth without poky gloom.

I am writing now.

'I am writing now.' This is a simple idea and even simpler phrase. But what exactly is happening as I write? At least three things.

First, I am considering my ideas, the abiding, anaemic copies of my experience. My consciousness is a rush of sensations, from colours and shapes to my own weight and position. But from this chaos, I abstract ideas, which

David Hume called 'the faint images of these in thinking'. Instead of the thrum and blur of life, these ideas are still and clear. (Falsely so, adds Alfred North Whitehead.)

Second, I am also trying to find the right words for these ideas, where 'right' means both true and pleasing. There is a duty to honesty and verity, yes. But I also want the phrases to be striking: interesting at worst, beautiful at best. This might be rhythm, a satisfying cadence of swiftness, slowness, and pause. It might be alliteration and assonance. It might be a surprising trope, something that burns the cornea, sharpening one's gaze a little. If the ideal prose is like a window, this is more like stained glass: transparent, but with a shape and colour of its own.

Third, I am scrawling aquamarine letters in a notebook. This is 'writing' in the technological sense, making marks. No trivial thing, text not only makes my private reflections public, but also encourages me to reflect at all. While communities cannot be neatly carved into 'primitive oral' and 'civilised literate' cuts, writing does have intellectual benefits. One is that it allows me to witness my words outside myself — to see them like things, to be held at arm's length and judged. In Europe at least, this helped to encourage philosophy. For all his caution about literacy, Plato was the beneficiary of this technology. And I am the beneficiary of this technology *and* this canon of thought.

Importantly, this third task typically withdraws from my consciousness. The pen and ink are 'ready-to-hand', as Heidegger once put it. They recede from inspection into intention. I do not concentrate on the nib and plunger; I do not need to will every curl and twirl of my wrist. Pen and paper are merely means to an end, guided by the logic Heidegger calls 'in-order-to'.

But as I compose now, I note that my words are fading — quite literally, the blue-green is becoming more pale. The nib scratches a little. My mind changes its focus, from literature to its paraphernalia. The ideas and words back off, and the pen appears again. Here, the instrument becomes what Heidegger calls 'present-at-hand': obtrusive, obvious, obstinate. The ready-to-hand 'takes its farewell', the philosopher wrote, 'in the conspicuousness of the unusable'.

And why is my pen suddenly unusable? I suspect it is running dry. It has a translucent panel immediately before the thread where the cap screws on, which becomes transparent in the light. And so I hold the pen up to the skylight to check. Sure enough, the panel is almost clear, so there are only a few drops left.

Yet I do not lower my hand. It stays raised above me, thumb and forefinger clasped gently on the instrument's middle. My head cocked slightly. I keep squinting and blinking.

I am sitting alone in a café, staring up at a pen.

A brief holiday

This is odd, I know.

I am *supposed* to simply check the little window. Then I am *supposed* to fill my pen from a bottle. Then I am *supposed* to allow all of the paraphernalia to recede from my reasoning again. The present-at-hand should give way quickly to the ready-to-hand.

Getting back to work would certainly be the ordinary choice, what Kant called the 'hypothetical imperative'. Here, all things are valued as the means to some end.

I need ink to make marks on paper, which creates a saleable manuscript, which earns money, which pays for new pens, ink, and paper. (I am a poor capitalist.) The logic here is straightforward: as equipment, the pen is either working or it is useless and so valueless. And likewise for me as a labourer. If I am looking at the pen, this must be because it helps me toil. If not, I am useless and so valueless.

Yet this is not my logic in the atrium. I continue to gaze at the drops of ink well beyond practicality. In fact, this 'well beyond' loses its meaning, because I forget about the minutes passing.

I am not staring because my pen has faults. The nib is not bent or the feed clogged. I am simply enjoying the way the liquid rolls in the barrel, the thin film it seems to leave briefly on the clear plastic, the gleam of its beryl against the grey-blue and black resin. The café has a great deal of ambient light, but the ink stands out for its shifting, gleaming aquamarine. Its hue and shade vary as my hand turns slowly, backwards and forwards, under the skylight.

I am looking at the pen for the sake of looking at the pen. My gesture suggests this commitment: *I am beholding this higher thing.*

Behold

This movement is part of a family of gestures I call the 'raised display'.

Here, we lift something to the careful gaze — and often to the light. Think of wine aficionados taking in the colours and textures of a fine syrah. The glass is not gripped at chest height, like a can of ale waiting to be guzzled. Instead, the drink is held up and away, where it can be contemplated before the first taste.

A similar gesture occurs in ceremonies, factual and fictional: from the crown held above the sitting monarch's head in Westminster Abbey, to Simba the cub shown off to the throng in *The Lion King*. If the crown and cub are not examined like wine, they are still glorified. These ceremonies need not involve royals. In a much-parodied moment in the film *Say Anything*, the lovesick John Cusack stands outside his girlfriend's bedroom and plays a song to win her back. The tune is for her, but the iconic boombox held aloft is for us — music itself is being exulted here. And this exaltation occurs above, where we often find worth in European culture. The lifted object has overcome gravity, the filth of mud and sweat, cramped existence; has become lighter, less weighed down by care.

Importantly, the raised display is not a salute or salutation. Both kinds of gesture use elevation and extension to invite our attention. But they ask different things of this concern. When we greet someone with a lifted hand or hat, we do not expect them to scrutinise the fingers or peak.

In the raised display, my hand becomes a plinth or dais: the object is held apart for inspection or recognition.

Aesthetics

Held in the gesture of raised display, my fountain pen is enjoyed aesthetically.

From the Greek 'aísthēsis' — or 'sensory perception'

— this is a very particular state of mind. It begins when I perceive an object, like the fluid in a cylinder. I find myself gratified or captivated by its features: the ink's bright blue, slow viscosity, even its tangy scent. These qualities are sensed, not simply thought. They draw me in, and I exercise my mind as I contemplate them curiously. Yet I also feel appropriated by the object, absorbed. As with games, I lose myself a little, along with my awareness of the clock.

The aesthetic object need not be art. In fact, art can be a distraction here. Some famous artworks are aesthetically dull: intellectually interesting but not perceptually inviting. Consider Marcel Duchamp's *Fountain*, which was actually a urinal. This made an enormous contribution to conceptual art — but was still just a urinal. And many aesthetic objects are not artificial, not 'made' in any meaningful sense. They can be anything that is literally attractive, anything that arrests my attention. The bright skylight atop the atrium's high bricks, making the tabletops gleam and offering a break from the near screen. In aísthēsis, my senses are engaged and enriched, and I welcome this — that is all.

And this is exactly how I am taking a short vacation from Kant's hypothetical imperative. If the pen is a means to the end of aesthetic experience, this aesthetic end is an end in itself. I do it to do it.

As I peer up at the almost-empty fountain pen, I am not concerned with my work. I am not worried about the manuscript in the literary market, which brings royalties, which buy stationery — and so on. In fact, I am not worried at all. Instead, I am celebrating the pen's gifts to sensation. The sensation *is* the celebration, and my gesture is its pose of observance.

The aesthete

Yet I am not sitting in a gallery, where aesthetic stares are encouraged. And I am not standing in awe of a Gothic cathedral or antipodean sunrise, weeping at the intimation of infinities. My pen is equipment: a stick for putting pigment on flat wood pulp. I am using it in an urban café, a site for business meetings and gossip. I am not supposed to be having an aesthetic experience in this place, at this time, with this thing.

Yes, if my pen were an artwork, this might be allowed. And any object *can* become an artwork if the right cohort welcomes it. As Arthur Danto argues, we need an 'artworld' to have special things called works of art. There have always been beautiful, striking, or otherwise sacred objects, objects set apart from ordinary life by their splendour or sophistication. Think of the Italian Renaissance humanist Petrarch, praising the handwriting in an earlier eleventh-century manuscript: 'majesty, harmony and sober decoration'. Think of the twelfth-century scribe Eadwine, praising himself: 'Neither my fame nor my praise will die quickly.' But works of fine art *as* works of fine art are a Renaissance invention, they did not exist until the visual arts gained professional prestige. Now, the artworld is somewhat free to decide what counts as art, artists, and success — it could easily do this for a stylish fountain pen.

But it has not. My pen is no artwork, and the café no museum. I am not writing as I ought to, not labouring studiously. Holding up my pen to the light, I am signalling a change of domain: from the utilitarian's to the aesthete's.

Symbols and the good

As an aesthetic object, my pen is a personal symbol.

Ordinary signs simply point to their signified, like the letters I scrawl in aquamarine then forget. They have little significance of their own, for writer or reader. Symbols nod beyond themselves like this, but they also nod to themselves. They have heft to them, a fullness that gives them power.

Pens suggest many things, from the obvious Freudian phallus, to perhaps the hope of literary immortality. For me, the pen is a symbol of the Good.

One of Plato's most famous arguments was that all things have their ideal reality, the Forms. These are the original reality, of which our everyday life is just a copy. Likewise, there are good things, but what they all have in common is goodness. For Plato, the ultimate Form of Forms is the Good, to which all true philosophers turn their gaze. This is a stubbornly visual theory, which John Dewey called the 'spectator conception of knowledge'. But it works here. For the Athenian, the Good is not something known, but that through which we know — the glow by which we see truly.

I am not a Platonist, but this idea of the Good appeals to me. Here, goodness is not a means to some other end — it is an end in itself. In fact, it is *the* end in itself. And as Plato observed, I have to withdraw from toil to glimpse its light.

This is exactly how I enjoy the pen aesthetically, as an invitation to the Good. Squinting up at the ink rolling in the barrel, I have a feeling of looking sincerely, of trying to see clearly, without convenient haste or lies. It takes effort, but this effort is enjoyable.

This is also how I write, when the writing is at its best: not as a tiny factory for the production of profitable phrases, but as an art that can be pursued patiently for its own sake.

My point is not that literature is useless — or that it ought to be. I can entertain or appal, can offer celebration or moral condemnation, can provide you with facts or fantasies. All these have some utility, if only psychological. While texts cannot simply tweak consciousness, they are certainly invitations to a change of mind. This is a use of sorts.

Yet I often cannot write this way. To gain clarity and beauty, I must forget you alongside the pen. I must put aside sales, praise, or awards. I must attend to the work, and I fail if this attention fails. The author Gene Wolfe puts this credo neatly: 'Success is continuing to write. Success is speaking in silence.' This is what the pretty pen means to me.

The held-up and gazed-upon pen is a symbol of its own best use.

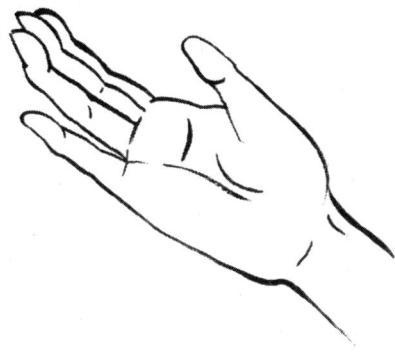

Hail

Let me speak again of ends, though not of finality.

Herakles died cruelly, even for a hero. He was mistakenly given a poisoned tunic by his second wife, the 'credulous' Deianira. The garment burned so savagely, he tore off his own skin. Ovid writes:

> Greedy flames sucked in his heart, dark
> perspiration poured from his whole frame,
> his scorched sinews crackled, and the hidden
> pestilence melted his bones. Raising his hands to
> the stars, he cried: 'O Juno, daughter of Saturn,
> feast your eyes upon my disasters: look down
> from on high upon my torment, and gaze your
> fill, till your barbarous heart is satisfied …'

Observe the lunk's mannerisms here, during his long, long agonies. Up his palms were lifted, up his look went — to the skies, his divine patrimony. This pose typically suggests Greek or Roman piety, prayers and thanks offered to those on high. But Herakles was mad with pain, rightly furious, panting with vengeance. This was not religious zeal; it was closer to blasphemy. With these hands, he was saying: *damn you, stepmother — and all like you.*

The same sign, but inverted: instead of invocation, invective.

So, not even the gods' movements are eternal and universal in their significance — not those they perform, not those they witness. These signs are fluid, subtle; they are finely suited to situations. And like the Olympians, our immortal gestures are changeful, even capricious. They outlive us, yes — but not through stiff fixity (another kind of death).

Speaking of which: back to the dying lug.

Herakles made himself a funeral pyre. Garlanded, he lay down with his club as a pillow, and had himself cremated. Or not quite himself. Jupiter had Vulcan slough off the mortal stuff, bubbling muscles, charred bones. What remained was godly, and his father carried this new divinity in a chariot to the stars. Herakles became a constellation.

Now Ovid adds one of my favourite lines in classical literature: 'Atlas felt the weight.' The author might have simply written that Herakles ascended to the skies — that he was a god now, and that was that. Instead, he gave this new collection of stars their own solidity. He wanted his readers to feel that new divine mass, weighing down upon poor Atlas.

Constellations are often seen as ethereal nothingness — just light, after all. And they are vague too. To the Greeks, this one suggested an anonymous kneeler, arm raised. Over two centuries before Ovid, the poet Aratus just knew it as 'a Phantom'. To the Chinese, it was part of the Celestial Market. To the Egyptians, it belonged to a large hippopotamus or bull. Pure symbolism, and hazy at that.

And yet, Atlas *felt* these new stars. Punished for warring against the Olympians, this Titan held up the skies. He had been transformed into a mountain range by Herakles' great-grandfather Perseus ('his bones became rock'). Atlas' brother Prometheus grieved for him, with that 'unwieldy load pressing upon his back'. Somehow, stellar Herakles was one load more. Another god up there, another burden pressing down.

This is a gestural observation: the language has heft. It is not that Platonic dream of pure form, in which truth can be stripped of stuff, in which the soul sheds its dross. We gesture with and within gravity.

And we also gesture within stories. To see Herakles is also to see Jupiter, Juno, Perseus, Atlas, Vulcan, and so on. The hero does not live discretely, as a single bit of information. He is incarnated and implicated, as are our signs of wonder or rage; our fingers to our lips, or fists to the skies.

Observe the double significance here. There is what the small, brief gesture tells us. Then there is what it invites us to discover, what exists heavily beyond our notice. We too can be Atlas, feeling the weight.

Geras

Herakles once bullied old age.

We see this on a two-handled, rounded jug from the fifth century before the common era. Tall and muscular, our hero looms over a stooped man with a walking stick: Geras, the personification of ageing. Geras is all wrong, his bulbous penis as thick as his ankles. This is against classical Greek taste. A man ought to have swollen muscles and slight cock, not the other way around.

Ugly, skinny Geras raises his free palm to Herakles in a gesture of supplication. He is pleading: *please accept me, keep me from harm, make me part of your life.* The old man cannot touch the hero's knees, chin, or hands in the usual way, so he simply reaches out. In this, he is no Greek hero — manly men do not beg. And the god-son seems to agree that this wizened thing is not worth his protection. Clasping the elder's little bald head, the brute raises his club high. Herakles will break these brittle bones, tear this thin skin.

And what is this story? We do not know. Yes, Herakles died then became young again with Hebe, goddess of youth. And yes, the literature of the Attic Greeks often celebrated youth over age. A lament from the chorus of Euripides' *Herakles*: 'Old age weighs me / Down worse than Etna's / Stones. It's drawn like a curtain / Between me and the sun.' It makes sense that the hairy lug takes a swing at senescence here. Still, the tale itself is lost. There are no plays, poems, dialogues — not even a rhetorical aside or anecdote in a memoir. All we know is that Geras was yet another of the hero's conquered monsters.

There is certainly little mystery to this daydream. Ageing destroys much. dignity, hope, knees. It is the stuff we are, continuing without regard to us. We leak, falter, shake — we lose our characteristic control and form. A century before the Geras jug was painted, the poet Theognis put this neatly: 'it goes / Fast as a dream, this honoured Youth, and Age, / The Shapeless Killer, hangs close over us.' Herakles beating Geras is the fantasy of vanquishing this Shapeless Killer; of wisdom and glory without wrinkle, drip, or droop; of a rich life without the cost of living.

But it is a fantasy.

Let Geras stand in for all that old age suggests. He is physicality, our existence through the flesh. He is ceaseless time, with its sundry rhythms. He is tradition, the shared ways of doing and thinking that we take up from the past (or not), and hand over to the future (or not). Herodotus, famously: 'Custom is king of all.' In other words, Geras is exactly what gestures arise from: our palpable situations of becoming. He is a symbol of the taken-for-granted worlds within which our movements make sense. And here is the elder, inviting the hero to join him, to participate in flesh, tempo, and society.

Perhaps, once upon a time, the lion-slayer did take Geras' hand. In the *Odyssey*, Homer put him in the underworld, just another sad shade lamenting his fate. There was no heroic escape from Hades, no conquering mortality. The hero saw Odysseus, wept, and told his story — then he left to join the other shadows. Resolving to die well at Troy, Achilles elsewhere said to his mother: 'not even Heracles fled his death, for all his power, / Fate crushed him, and Hera's savage anger.' For Homer, Herakles was *dead* dead.

The strutting hero on the jug will not accept this reality. With characteristic violence, he snubs Geras and the very mortal universe he represents. There will be no clasped hand of fellowship, no address of intimacy. He will touch the old man only from a distance — and with a knotted cudgel.

That is to say, Herakles refuses Geras' gesture, while I welcome it. This work is my curious hail in reply.

A Curt Nod

One of the small satisfactions of civilised life is casual public acknowledgement.

I know nothing of the stooping shuffler in the plaid cloth cap with his panting Pekinese; of the cyclist, moustache thick above his thin wet school uniform; of the strider in faux-leopard sneakers screaming at her phone above the screaming southerly — but I greet each of them, and they me.

Raised eyebrows. A low wave. Perhaps even a gentle smile.

This might be trivialised as politeness — and politeness it is. But it makes life slightly easier. We are not making friends or trying to flirt. This is not an introduction or farewell — not yet. Instead, we are maintaining the stuff that these intimacies arise from: mutual acknowledgement. We need not flail or scream to have ourselves felt or heard. The nod says: *you and I, we are in a common world*.

In this spirit, I nod here to some of the works that inspired or informed this work. I want to recognise them as part of a shared literary neighbourhood — so that you might get to know them better (with glee or suspicion) or simply pass them by.

This list is very partial, in both senses of the word: piecemeal and prejudiced. The full list of endnotes is absurdly long, and my editors baulk at its bulk. Here, I am simply tipping my cap to some notables.

Gobsmacked

If this work has a patron genius, it is that of Roberto Calasso. I cannot claim even a fraction of his learning, and his style is his own. But I am drawn to his sense of immensity and intricacy, to his spiralling logic, to his naked curiosity. I recommend Calasso's *The Marriage of Cadmus and Harmony*, translated by Tim Parks (London: Vintage Books, 1994) and *Ardor*, translated by Richard Dixon (London: Allen Lane, 2014).

The drawing of Herakles gobsmacked is by the Group of Boston 00.348, terracotta column-krater, 360 CE, held in the Metropolitan Museum of New York.

On my way to gestures, I was guided by these luminaries: Adam Kendon, *Gesture: Visible Action as Utterance* (Cambridge: Cambridge University Press, 2004); David McNeill, *Hand and Mind: What Gestures Reveal About Thought* (Chicago: University of Chicago Press, 1992); Susan Goldin-Meadow, *Hearing Gesture: How Our Hands Help Us Think* (Cambridge: Harvard University Press, 2005). I also read several of Cornelia Müller's excellent papers, including 'Gesture and Sign: Cataclysmic Break or Dynamic Relations?', *Frontiers in Psychology*, 9 (2018), p. 1651.

The foremost twentieth-century philosopher of embodiment is Maurice Merleau-Ponty, and his opus *Phenomenology of Perception* is the best starting point for anyone curious. I have the older translation by Colin Smith (London: Routledge & Kegan Paul, 1970). On the ways our bodies nudge and shove our ideas, see also George Lakoff and Mark Johnson, *Metaphors We Live By* (Chicago: The University of Chicago Press, 1980).

Alfred North Whitehead's work is a constant reminder to be wary of false clarity. His *Modes of Thought* (New York: Capricorn Books, 1958) is a succinct introduction.

Tally Up

Erving Goffman's *Encounters* (Harmondsworth: Penguin University Books, 1961) is a brilliantly observed account of social events *as* events — as happenings, with their own unities.

Centuries on, Karl Marx's description of the alienation of labour remains illuminating and surprisingly moving. My edition is *The Economic & Philosophic Manuscripts of 1844*, edited by Dirk J. Struik, translated by Martin Milligan (New York: International Publishers, 1969).

David Harvey has much to teach about Marx — and about our capitalist era. If you are keen, begin with his *The Condition of Postmodernity* (Oxford: Blackwell, 1997).

Well? And? So?

The antisemitic caricature of the 'Jewish' shrug comes from *Inscribed Postcard of a Shrugging Jewish Man in a Yellow Hat*, 1905, The United States Holocaust Memorial Museum.

On 'antisemitism' against 'anti-Semitism' or the like, see Deborah E. Lipstadt, *Antisemitism: Here and Now* (Melbourne: Scribe Publications, 2019), pp. 22–5. 'Something this absurd does not deserve a capital letter.'

As literature, the Bible is iffy: by turns sublime, petty, dull. If you cannot stomach its moralities, you might still savour its dubious but elegant King James English. I own a little pocket edition, *The Holy Bible Containing the Old and New Testaments* (Oxford: Oxford University Press), though I check other translations and commentaries for scholarship. My selections from the Talmud are from the edition translated by Norman Solomon (London: Penguin Classics, 2009), and my edition of the Qur'an is translated by M.A.S. Abdel Haleem (Oxford: Oxford University Press, 2008).

Augustine's memoir is a spiritual adventure, taking the Roman from horny, proud youth to flaccid, humbled age. I need not agree with his later piety to be fascinated by his life. See his *Confessions*, translated by Henry Chadwick (Oxford: Oxford University Press, 2008).

Jean-Paul Sartre was not Jewish, but his *Anti-Semite and Jew*, translated by George J. Becker (New York: Schocken Books, 1976) is a classic existentialist study of antisemitism.

In his *People of the Book: Canon, Meaning, and Authority* (Cambridge: Harvard University Press, 1997), Moshe Halbertal offers a nuanced picture of Jewishness and textuality.

I enjoyed Ted Cohen's brief *Jokes: Philosophical Thoughts on Joking Matters* (Chicago: University of Chicago Press, 2001). It exemplifies wit by talking about humour while also being humorous.

Despite my sympathy for existentialism, I think Simone de Beauvoir's *The Ethics of Ambiguity*, translated by Bernard Frechtman (New York: Philosophical Library, 2015) falls short of its own target. It remains a fine and finely written manifesto.

Ply, Pliant, Pliable

The illustration that begins this chapter is by Hilaire-Germain-Edgar Degas, *Plié in Second Position at the Barre*, 1878, Harvard Art.

In her *Apollo's Angels: A History of Ballet* (London: Granta, 2010), Jennifer Homas offers a light-footed story of her art. Without this work, I would have stumbled far more.

I appreciated Renée K. Nicholson's honesty about dance (and herself) in 'Five Positions', *The Gettysburg Review*, 2007, pp. 369–81. She puts her ambivalence well.

Simone de Beauvoir's *The Second Sex*, translated by H.M. Parshley (Harmondsworth: Penguin Books, 1972) is not up to date on the physical and social sciences. And there is a little too much Freud, like a gymnastic vault Beauvoir had to grip then leap over. But her observations about patriarchy are powerful and prescient.

Unclean, Undead

Trust is a muddy idea that Karen Jones cleans up philosophically in 'Trustworthiness', *Ethics*, 123.1 (2012), pp. 61–85.

My debt to Mary Douglas is obvious. Her *Purity and Danger: An Analysis of Concept of Pollution and Taboo* (London: Routledge, 2002) is a classic of its kind. (And like all classics, the criticisms continue.)

I know of no better analysis of symbols than Paul Ricoeur's *The Symbolism of Evil*, translated by Emerson Buchanan (Boston: Beacon Press, 1969). It invited me to see interpretation anew.

As a theorist, Jean-Paul Sartre has a wonderful first-person touch. See his discussion of slime in *Being and Nothingness*, translated by Hazel Barnes (New York: Philosophical Library, 1956), pp. 604–12.

Yes, more Erving Goffman. His *Stigma: Notes on the Management of Spoiled Identity* (New York: Simon & Schuster, 1986) is a patient and humane look at outsiders.

Fascinating

Benjamin D. Sommer's *The Bodies of God and the World of Ancient Israel* (Cambridge: Cambridge University Press, 2009) is a reminder of the glorious messiness of the historical Israelite god, and of how much we lose when we tidy this up theologically.

For atheists interested in the numinous, I recommend Rudolf Otto's *The Idea of the Holy*, translated by John W. Harvey (Oxford: Oxford University Press, 1958). For my own thoughts on this: Damon A. Young, 'Being Grateful for Being: Being, Reverence, and Finitude', *Sophia*, 44.2 (2005), pp. 31–53.

Manu Saadia is a Trekker and an economist, and his *Trekonomics* (San Francisco: Pipertext Publishing, 2016) is the best of both worlds.

Jorge Luis Borges is marvellous on translation — and on reading in general. My edition of his essays is *The Total Library: Non-Fiction 1922–1986*, edited by Eliot Weinberger, translated by Esther Allen, Suzanne Jill Levine, and Eliot Weinberger (London: Penguin Books, 2001).

Horns

Amica Lykiardopoulos provides a helpful overview of the malicious look in 'The Evil Eye: Towards an Exhaustive Study', *Folklore*, 92.2 (1981), pp. 221–30.

On the human logic behind apotropaic signs, I enjoyed Christa Sütterlin's 'Universals in Apotropaic Symbolism: A Behavioral and Comparative Approach to Some Medieval Sculptures', *Leonardo*, 22.1 (1989), pp. 65–74.

In 'Ten Ways to Interpret Ritual Hand Gestures', *Studia Antiqua*, 12.1 (2013), David M. Calabro shows how different ancient gestures can be understood *differently*. A good warning against scholarly narrowness.

Paul Harvey's *The Oxford Companion to Classical Literature* is a wonderful compendium. I regularly dip in and out, and my old paperback (Oxford: Oxford University Press, 1984) is frayed and buckling.

The anonymous engraving with the gleefully wayward wife is *Cuckolded Husband Rocks Cradle While Wife Smokes*, 1628, The Folger Shakespeare Library.

Pew Pew Pew

Takie Lebra gives a careful but suggestive account of Japanese quiet in 'The Cultural Significance of Silence in Japanese Communication', in *Identity, Gender, and Status in Japan* (Leiden: Brill, 2007), pp. 115–26.

Apologies for the wall of academic papers, but this chapter makes little sense without their load-bearing:

D. Hemenway, D. Azrael, and M. Miller, 'Gun Use in the United States: Results from Two National Surveys', *Injury Prevention*, 6.4 (2000), p. 263; Matthew J. Lacombe, Adam J. Howat, and Jacob E. Rothschild, 'Gun Ownership as a Social Identity: Estimating Behavioral and Attitudinal Relationships', *Social Science Quarterly*, 100 (2019), pp. 2408–24; Nicholas Buttrick, 'Protective Gun Ownership as a Coping Mechanism', *Perspectives on Psychological Science*, 15.4 (2020), pp. 835–55; Wolfgang Stroebe, N. Pontus Leander, and Arie W. Kruglanski, 'Is It a Dangerous World Out There? The Motivational Bases of American Gun Ownership', *Personality and Social Psychology Bulletin*, 43.8 (2017), pp. 1071–85; Michael C. Gearhart and others, 'Fear of Crime, Racial Bias, and Gun Ownership', *Health & Social Work*, 44.4 (2019), pp. 241–48.

Debate continues about the methodologies of Dave Grossman's *On Killing: The Psychological Cost of Learning to Kill in War and Society* (London: Back Bay Books, 1996). But the work is a troubling reminder of the (often uncounted) tithe that so many (often unwilling) killers pay.

You need not read about Don Quixote for the hidalgo's mockery of mosqueteros; the picaresque novel also features everything from slapstick and whimsy to romance and tragedy. My fancy clothbound edition with Coralie Bickford-Smith's cheery designs is Miguel de Cervantes, *The Ingenious Hidalgo Don Quixote de La Mancha*, translated by John Rutherford (London: Penguin Classics, 2018).

Shush

The first statuette from my time-travelling is *A Child God, Probably Harpokrates*, first century BCE or before, Metropolitan Museum of New York. The second is *Harpokrates (Horus the Child)*, 664–342 BCE, The Walters Art Museum.

W.R. Elton offers a vivid intellectual portrait of Shakespearean England in 'Shakespeare and the Thought of His Age', in *The Cambridge Companion to Shakespeare Studies*, edited by S. Wells (Cambridge: Cambridge University Press, 1997), pp. 17–34.

I like how Alexandra von Lieven traces the outlines of wandering divinities in 'Translating Gods, Interpreting Gods', in *Greco-Egyptian Interactions*, edited by Ian Rutherford (Oxford: Oxford University Press, 2016), pp. 61–82. A warning against pious fetishism.

Friedrich Nietzsche's *The Gay Science* is a favourite of mine, chiefly for its cheer, its smile at the abyss. My edition is translated by Walter Kaufmann (New York: Vintage Books, 1974).

Gills, Glass

I owe much to Michel Foucault's idea of subjectivity, to the idea that we need not be governed when we are taught to govern ourselves. You can read more in Essential Works of Foucault, vol. 1: *Ethics: Subjectivity and Truth*, edited by Paul Rabinow (London: Penguin Books, 2000), pp. 23–79. But as I acknowledge my intellectual debt to Foucault, I must also acknowledge the claims against him: Matthew Campbell, 'French Philosopher Michel Foucault "Abused Boys in Tunisia"', *The Sunday Times*, 28 March 2021.

Anna Marie Roos' *Goldfish* (London: Reaktion Books, 2019) is something Proust might have enjoyed: a miniature, full of truths and beauties.

Thomas Nagel's thought experiment is still challenging: 'What Is It Like to Be a Bat?', in *Mortal Questions* (Cambridge: Cambridge University Press, 2013), pp. 165–80.

I learned a great deal about other animals' worlds from Jakob von Uexküll, *A Foray Into the Worlds of Animals and Humans*, translated by Joseph D. O'Neil (Minneapolis: University of Minneapolis Press, 2010), p. 45. Alas, Uexküll was also a nationalist, a bigot, and a critic of democracy. On this, see: Carlo Brentari, *Jakob von Uexküll: The Discovery of the Umwelt between Biosemiotics and Theoretical Biology* (New York: Springer, 2015), pp. 38–42.

Savage Noble

You can read my brief celebration of swords in 'Why Are Swords Still a Thing?', *Meanjin*, 77.4 (2018), pp. 10–12. On the martial arts and courtesy, see my 'Bowing to Your Enemies: Courtesy, Budō, and Japan', *Philosophy East and West*, 59.2 (2009), pp. 188–215.

Samuel Pepys' diary has such immediacy to it. Living history, with all its idiosyncrasies. My edition is *The Diary of Samuel Pepys: A Selection*, edited by Robert Latham and William Matthews (London: Penguin Books, 2003).

Stephen Hand taught me nearly everything (good) I know about historical fencing. To learn more about Renaissance broadsword combat, try Hand's *English Swordsmanship: The True Fight of George Silver* (Highland Village: Chivalry Bookshelf, 2006).

Three helpful works on the duel in history: François Billacois, *The Duel*, translated by Trista Selous (New Haven: Yale University Press, 1990), V.G. Kiernan, *The Duel in European History* (Oxford: Oxford University Press, 1989), and Robert Baldick, *The Duel* (London: Spring Books, 1965).

The Protestant work ethic has become a cliché, but Max Weber's thesis is both more subtle and more surprising than the phrase suggests. See *The Protestant Ethic and the Spirit of Capitalism*, translated by Talcott Parsons (London: Routledge, 2001).

Hello There

I always find Ludwig Wittgenstein challenging — like the grit challenges the oyster. An excellent collection of his ideas on art, culture, and morality is *Culture and Value*, edited by G.H. von Wright, translated by Peter Winch (Chicago: University of Chicago Press, 1984). 'The book is full of life — not like a man, but like an ant-heap.' (p. 62)

Julia M.H. Smith offers a brilliant picture of so-called 'dark ages' in *Europe After Rome: A New Cultural History 500–1000* (Oxford: Oxford University Press, 2005).

For a much gloomier portrait, see Catherine Nixey on the Christian destruction of antiquity: *The Darkening Age* (London: Pan Books, 2017).

If you want to visit the wretched hive of scum and villainy of *Star Wars* philosophy, try these papers to start with: Matt Hummel, '"You Are Asking Me to Be Rational": Stoic Philosophy and the Jedi Order', in *The Ultimate Star Wars and Philosophy: You Must Unlearn What You Have Learned*, edited by Jason T. Eberl and Kevin S. Decker (Malden: John Wiley & Sons, 2015), pp. 20–30; William A. Lindenmuth, 'The Jedi Knights of Faith: Anakin, Luke, and Soren (Kierkegaard)', in *The Ultimate Star Wars and Philosophy*, pp. 31–41.

Originally a sceptic about the therapeutic use of nostalgia, I was persuaded by these papers: Joost Leunissen and others, 'The Hedonic Character of Nostalgia: An Integrative Data Analysis', *Emotion Review*, 13.2 (2021), pp. 139–5; Andrew A. Abeyta, Clay Routledge, and Samuel Kaslon, 'Combating Loneliness with Nostalgia: Nostalgic Feelings Attenuate Negative Thoughts and Motivations Associated with Loneliness',

Frontiers in Psychology, 11 (2020), p. 1219; Erica G. Hepper and others, 'Time Capsule: Nostalgia Shields Psychological Wellbeing from Limited Time Horizons', *Emotion*, 21.3 (2021), pp. 644–64; Clay Routledge and others, 'The Power of the Past: Nostalgia as a Meaning-Making Resource', *Memory*, 20.5 (2012), pp. 452–60.

If you are seeking sophisticated historical fiction, I recommend these marvels on medieval France, imperial Rome, and Edo Japan: Umberto Eco, *The Name of the Rose*, translated by William Weaver (London: Vintage Books, 2004); Marguerite Yourcenar, *Memoirs of Hadrian*, translated by Paul Bailey (London: Penguin Modern Classics, 2001); Shūsako Endō, *Silence*, translated by William Johnston (New York: Picador, 2016).

Aiki

Jeanette Bicknell offers a clear overview of aesthetics and the martial arts in 'Aesthetics of the Martial Arts', *Philosophy Compass*, 16.5 (2021), pp. 1–8.

Putting aside the talk of happiness, Mihaly Csikszentmihalyi's work on flow is liberating. My edition is *Flow: The Classic Work on How to Achieve Happiness* (London: Rider, 2002). For a fascinating cross-cultural discussion of flow: Kevin Krein and Jesus Ilundain, 'Mushin and Flow: An East-West Comparative Analysis', in *Philosophy and the Martial Arts: Engagement*, edited by Graham Priest and Damon Young (London: Taylor & Francis Group), pp. 139–64.

Jigoro Kano was a martial artist but also a modern educationalist. You get a strong sense of both talents in *Kodokan Judo* (New York: Kodansha International, 1994).

Kevin S.Y. Tan provides an excellent critique of the martial arts mythos in 'Constructing a Martial Tradition: Rethinking a Popular History of Karate-Dou', *Journal of Sport and Social Issues*, 28.2 (2004), pp. 169–92.

Edward W. Said's *Orientalism* (London: Penguin Books, 2019) is as damning as it is disturbingly current.

Catching the Light

On the basic idea of aesthetic encounters, Monroe C. Beardsley is fantastic: 'Aesthetic Experience', in *The Aesthetic Point of View*, edited by Michael J. Wreen and Donald M. Callen (Ithaca: Cornell University Press, 1982), pp. 285–87. For a less academic approach, try Mihaly Csikszentmihalyi and Rick Robinson's, *The Art of Seeing* (Santa Monica: Getty Center for Education in the Arts, 1990).

Whitehead once wrote that European philosophy is just footnotes to Plato. A quip, but a fair one. If you want to encounter Plato's (maddening) intelligence, artistry, and vision, his works are freely available in many translations. I have this single hardbound edition with various translators: *Plato: The Collected Dialogues*, edited by Edith Hamilton and Huntington Cairns (Princeton: Princeton University Press, 1996).

For a fuller history of the rise of the fine arts during the Renaissance, see Michael Baxandall, *Painting and Experience in Fifteenth-Century Italy* (Oxford: Oxford University Press, 1972). A classic study of art as a social and economic achievement, rather than simply an aesthetic one. For more on this in modern France, see Pierre Bourdieu's *Distinction*, translated by Richard Nice (London: Routledge & Kegan Paul, 1986).

Hail

The portrait of Herakles and Geras is from Geras Painter, *Pelike*, 480–470 BCE, Louvre Museum, Département des Antiquités grecques, étrusques et romaines.

I cannot speak to Ovid's Latin, but his work in translation is by turns stirring, amusing, and troubling. I have the Penguin edition: Publius Ovidius Naso, *The Metamorphoses of Ovid*, translated by Mary M. Innes (London: 1979).

On the Greeks and the tragedy of ageing, see Philip S. Miller, 'Old Age in the Greek Poets', *The Classical Weekly*, 48.13 (1955), pp. 177–82; Chris Gilleard, 'Old Age in Ancient Greece: Narratives of Desire, Narratives of Disgust', *Journal of Aging Studies*, 21.1 (2007), pp. 81–92. For the more sympathetic illustrations on Attic vases, see Susan B. Matheson's 'Old Age in Athenian Vase-Painting', in *Athenian Potters and Painters*, edited by John H. Oakley and Olga Palagia (Oxford: Oxbow Books, 2009), pp. ii, 192–200.

Homer's *Iliad* is a thrilling epic with familiar emotions but foreign values. I like Robert Fagles' loose, urgent modern translation, though you need not have my fancy illustrated edition (London: The Folio Society, 1996).

Gestures of Thanks

I nod gratefully to my agents at Zeitgeist Agency, Benython Oldfield and Sharon Galant. Without them, I flail.

Once again, I salute everyone at Scribe, especially founder Henry Rosenbloom and publisher Molly Slight. A fist bump to Sarah Braybrooke for commissioning this work and to Simon Wright for his suggestions. To copyeditor David Golding, I press my hands together in thanks: you slayed those semicolons valiantly. I also tip my hat to cover designer Laura Thomas for giving my hand-waving a face, and to Angi Thomas for the illustrations.

I raise my sword to the following for sharing their expertise: Guy Windsor, Cass Frances, Steve Colangelo, Iwan Pranatio, John Birmingham, Alan Baxter, Jeanette Bicknell, Sarah Ross, Raúl Sánchez García, Gerhild Grabitzer, Peter Grandbois, Daryl Adair, Kim Haines-Eitzen, Arran Gare, Bryan van der Norden, James Elkins, Cornelia Müller, Doris Srinivasan, Jacob Latham, Deena Weinstein, Adrian Poruciuc, Caitríona Devery, Stu Willis.

And high-five to Malcolm Jones for going above and beyond on the mano cornuta.

I clink my coffee cup to the whole gang from Villino and Ecru, and also to John from Daci & Daci: gracias por tus cafés y conversaciones, parcero. Este manuscrito contiene muchas tazas llenas.

Shastra Deo wrote a perfect poem for my epigraph, and I bow to her — and to her generous talent.

After every riverside chat and café catechism and kitchen debate, a long, long hug for Ruth Quibell. Our fingers are clasped.

And to my children nearby, shouting at friends elsewhere: I put my finger to my lips.